"THE MUSIC OF THE FUTURE,"

A LETTER TO M. FRÉDÉRIC VILLOT,

BY

RICHARD WAGNER.

TRANSLATED FROM THE ORIGINAL GERMAN

BY

EDWARD DANNREUTHER.

———◆———

LONDON

Travis & Emery Music Bookshop

Richard Wagner

The Music of the Future.

Translated by Edward Dannreuther

Facsimile of the London 1873 edition.

Republished Travis & Emery 2010.

Published by
Travis & Emery Music Bookshop
17 Cecil Court, London, WC2N 4EZ, United Kingdom.
(+44) 20 7240 2129
neworders@travis-and-emery.com

Hardback: 978-1-84955-082-6
Paperback: 978-1-84955-083-3

"THE MUSIC OF THE FUTURE,"

A LETTER TO M. FRÉDÉRIC VILLOT,

BY

RICHARD WAGNER.

TRANSLATED FROM THE ORIGINAL GERMAN

BY

EDWARD DANNREUTHER.

———◆———

LONDON:

SCHOTT & CO., 159, REGENT STREET.

Brussells:	*New York:*	*Paris:*
SCHOTT FRÈRES,	T. SCHIRMER,	MAISON SCHOTT,
82, Montagne de la Cour.	701, Broadway.	6, Rue du Hazard.

1873.

Price One Shilling.

"THE MUSIC OF THE FUTURE."

"THE MUSIC OF THE FUTURE,"

A LETTER TO M. FRÉDÉRIC VILLOT,

BY

RICHARD WAGNER.

TRANSLATED FROM THE ORIGINAL GERMAN

BY

EDWARD DANNREUTHER.

———◆———

LONDON:

SCHOTT & CO., 159, REGENT STREET.

Brussells:	*New York:*	*Paris:*
SCHOTT FRÈRES,	T. SCHIRMER,	MAISON SCHOTT,
82, Montagne de la Cour.	701, Broadway.	6, Rue du Hazard.

——

1873.

TRANSLATOR'S NOTE.

———◆———

SOME time previous to the production of "Tannhäuser" at the Grand Opéra, this essay was first published in French, under the title of "*Quatre Poêmes d'Opéra, précédés d'une Lettre sur la Musique*. Paris : Bourdillat & Cie. 1861." It formed the introduction to a prose translation of the poems to "Der fliegende Holländer," "Tannhäuser," "Lohengrin," and "Tristan und. Isolde.' The original German copy was subsequently published as a separate pamphlet : "*Zukunftsmusik, Brief an einen französischen Freund :* Leipzig, Weber, 1861;" and has lately been included in its author's "*Gesammelte Schriften, vol. VII.* Leipzig : Fritzsch. 1873."

The translator has as wholesome a horror of loose paraphrase as of macerating the Queen's English; and whilst striving to attain a readable version, he has tried to be strictly faithful to Wagner's teutonic diction and construction.

DEAR FRIEND,

You wished me to furnish a clear exposition of the ideas on art I published in Germany some years ago, the nature of which is such as to have created both sensation and vexation enough to prepare for me in France a reception full of expectant curiosity. You deemed a short and concise exposition advisable, and kindly expressed a hope that it might tend to remove much error and prejudice, and thus enable one or the other timorous critic, at the impending performance of one of my dramatic-musical productions, to form a correct judgment of the work *per se*, without reference to any apparently doubtful theory.

By desiring at the same time that I should place a translation of my operatic poems before the French public, you have shown me the only way in which I believe it possible to comply with your request, and have enabled me to undertake a task which I should otherwise have found exceedingly difficult. For it would have been impossible for me again to thread a labyrinth of theoretical speculation in purely abstract form ; and by the great disinclination I feel towards merely re-reading my theoretical writings, I perceive that at the time when I conceived them I must have been in an *abnormal* state, such as an artist may well experience once, but rarely twice, in a lifetime. To begin with, let me sketch the outlines of this state, as I now perceive them. If you will grant me some little space for this, I may hope to show you the concrete contents of my artistic theories by starting with a description of my subjective frame of mind—for to repeat these theories in an abstract form would be to frustrate the object of my communication, and would, besides, be nearly impossible to me.

If all nature, looked upon from the widest point of view,

may be considered as a consecutive development from uncon-
sciousness to consciousness, a progress which is most strikingly
apparent in human individuals, it may be found especially
interesting to observe such a process in the life of artists, for
in them and in their creations the world represents itself and
attains consciousness.

With an artist, too, the shape-giving and representing impulse
is, of its nature, entirely instinctive and unconscious; even
where he requires reflection in order to mature the type of his
intuition into an objective work of art, the definite choice of
his means of expression will not so much be determined by
conscious thought as by that spontaneous intuition which constitutes the character of his individual genius. He will not feel
the necessity of continuous reflection until he meets with a
considerable impediment in applying the requisite means of
expressing his idea—that is to say, at the moment when he
feels that the means for the representation of his artistic idea
are insufficient, or perhaps utterly wanting. The latter will
more especially be the case of an artist who for the realisation
of his idea depends not alone on inanimate instruments, but
upon a combination of living artistic powers as well. Now,
such a combination in the very widest sense is absolutely
necessary to the dramatist who aims at a perfectly intelligible
representation of his poem; for to attain this end he requires
the stage, which, including all the arts of representation, with
heir peculiar laws, is in itself a perfectly distinct branch of art.
Approaching the stage, then, the dramatist finds in it a "ready-
made" element of art; in order to see his artistic idea realized,
he must amalgamate himself with it, and with all its peculiarities.
If the dramatic poet's tendencies are in perfect accordance
with those of the stage, there can be no occasion for the conflict
I hint at, and in order to determine the value of the work
produced, we have only to consider the character of this
accordance. If, on the other hand, these tendencies diverge
radically, it is easy to imagine the difficulty and distress
experienced by an artist who finds himself compelled to employ

for the exposition of artistic ends an organization which was originally devoted to a totally different purpose.

Having at a certain period of my life gained the conviction that I was suffering in such a false position, I felt constrained to stop in a career of more or less unconscious artistic production, and, by means of mature reflection, to master the intellectual aspect of my problematic situation. I think I may assume that no artist before me has ever been so deeply impressed by this problem as myself, for the artistic elements brought into play in my case have never encountered each other in a manner so varied and so peculiar. It was necessary to conciliate poetry and music on the one side with the most contestable, the most equivocal public art-institution of our day—the opera—on the other.

Permit me first to point out a difference, most important to my thinking, between the position of operatic composers and librettists as regards the opera in France and Italy and the position which they occupy towards it in Germany. This difference is so considerable, that as soon as I lay its characteristics before you, it will be evident why the above-mentioned problem should have been felt so intensely by a German artist only.

In Italy, where the opera first developed itself, the musician's task has ever consisted in little or nothing beyond writing a number of airs for certain singers, whose dramatic talents were of less than secondary importance. These airs were simply intended to give the singers a chance of displaying their specific vocal dexterity. The poem and the scene served no purpose beyond providing this exhibition of vocal virtuosi with a pretext for time and place; the singer gave way to the dancer, who danced just what the other had sung, and the composer's task consisted simply in furnishing variations on the same type of *aria*. Here, then, we have perfect accordance up to the most minute detail, as the composer invariably wrote for certain special singers, whose individuality pointed out to him the character of the required variations. Thus Italian opera became quite a separate "genre" of art, which, having nothing to do with the veritable drama, remained, properly speaking, alien to music as well ; and from the prosperity of opera in Italy the art-student will date the decline of music in that country : an assertion which will readily be received by those who have any conception of the grandeur, the wealth, and the ineffable depth of earlier · Italian church music, and who, for instance, after hearing Palestrina's "Stabat Mater," will never dream of maintaining that Italian opera can be looked upon as the legitimate daughter of that wondrous mother. Merely men-·tioning this by the way, let us for our immediate purpose only keep the fact in view that in Italy up to this day there exists a perfect accordance between the tendencies of the operatic stage and those of operatic composers.

Nor are these relations altered in France, only the task. has here become greater for the singer as well as for the composer ; since the dramatic poet's co-operation came to be of very much greater importance than in Italy. In accordance with the character of the nation, and with an important, immediately preceding, development of dramatic poetry and mimetics, the exigencies of dramatic art gave laws to opera. At the " Grand Opera," a distinct style was developed, derived in its leading features from the rules of the " Théatre Français," and including all the conventions and requirements of a dramatic performance. Without for the present intending to characterise it more closely, let us only remember the fact that a *model* theatre existed, where this style developed itself authoritatively for both actor and author, so that the author found a clearly-defined outline which he was to fill with action and music, keeping in mind the special well-trained singers and actors with whom he found himself in perfect accordance as far as his artistic purpose was concerned.

The opera reached Germany as a finished foreign production, essentially alien to the character of the nation. In the first instance, German princes invited Italian opera companies and composers to their courts. German composers had to migrate to Italy to learn the trick of composing operas. Later, the theatres began to introduce German versions of *French* operas. The attempts at *German* opera consisted simply in imitations of foreign operas in the German language. A central model theatre for this purpose was never established. An Italian style, a French style, and German imitations of both, existed side by side in perfect anarchy; and in addition to these, attempts were made at forming an independent and popular "genre" out of the original, hitherto but little developed, "Singspiel" (Vaudeville); but, naturally enough, such attempts were almost invariably stifled by the foreign productions, which were at all events more finished in form.

The most palpable evil arising from these conflicting influences was the utter absence of all method and style in operatic *performances*. In less populous towns, where the audience was small and but rarely changing, managers thought fit, in order to vary the attraction of the repertoire, to compel the selfsame singers to sing in quickest succession tragic or comic French, Italian, or German operas—the latter either imitated from both the former, or derived from the lowest class of *vaudeville*. Works that had been composed for the most distinguished Italian virtuosi, and with special consideration for their individual capacities, were undertaken by singers devoid of all vocal ability and training, and ludicrously screamed in a language diametrically opposed in character to that of Italy.

French operas, whose effect depended entirely upon a pathetic declamation of strongly-marked rhetorical phrases, were performed in translations hurriedly manufactured by literary hacks, mostly without the slightest consideration for the connection between music and declamation, and with the most horrifying incorrectness of prosody; a circumstance in itself sufficient to preclude the formation of a healthy style of delivery, making both singer and audience alike heedless of the text. Hence imperfection in all directions—nowhere a leading model theatre conducted on intelligent principles—a total absence of training, or at least an insufficient cultivation of voices—everywhere complete artistic anarchy.

You will agree with me that to a true and earnest musician such an operatic theatre had in reality no existence. If by inclination or education a composer was drawn to the stage, he necessarily preferred writing Italian operas for Italy or French operas for France; and whilst Mozart and Gluck composed French and Italian operas, the really national music of Germany grew on foundations' totally different from the operatic genre. Quite apart from the opera, *German* music, starting from that branch of the art which the Italians deserted on the first appearance of opera, developed itself from Bach to Beethoven, attained its wondrous wealth, and rose to its acknowledged universal importance.

Thus the German musician, looking up from his own field —that of instrumental and choral music—saw no finished and imposing form in the operatic "genre"—he found nothing which in its relative perfection might have served him as a model, such as he found ready in those branches of the art which were perfectly his own. Whilst the oratorio and the symphony presented a nobly finished form, the opera only offered a disconnected mass of small and undeveloped shapes, encumbered by conventionalities quite incomprehensible to him and most inimical to all freedom of development. To grasp my meaning clearly, compare the broad and richly developed forms of a symphony by Beethoven with the movements in his opera "Fidelio;" you perceive at once how hampered the master felt here, how he scarcely ever reached a full development of his power, and how he therefore, as if irresistibly driven to seek an outlet for the abundance of his thought, threw himself with all his might upon the overture, and produced in it a musical work of hitherto unknown breadth and importance. Disheartened by this single attempt at an opera, he gave it up, without, however, entirely resigning the wish to find a poem which might give him an opportunity of unfolding his entire musical power. He had a vision of "*the Ideal.*"

As opera was in reality presented to the German musician, it appeared so problematic and unsatisfactory, now attracting, now repelling him, that he could not avoid ultimately finding an ideal direction for it; and herein consists the peculiar significance of German artistic efforts, not only in this but in every other field of art. Allow me to describe this significance a little more clearly.

It is indisputable that the Romance nations of Europe had at an early period attained a considerable superiority over the Germanic nations in the development of FORM. Italy, Spain, and France created both in life and in art a form which was in unison with their nature and charming in itself, and which soon received a generally valid and legitimate application to all expressions of their life and their art; whilst Germany remained in an undeniable state of anarchy, which was scarcely hidden by the attempts to use ready-made foreign forms, but was in fact rather aggravated thereby. The evident disadvantage in which the Germanic nation was placed in all that regarded form (and what does *not* regard it!) very naturally retarded the development of German art and literature for so long a period that it was not till the middle of the last century that Germany first saw a movement similar to that which the Romance nations had already experienced, ever since the time of the Renaissance. This German movement could in the first instance only assume the character of a reaction against the foreign, distorted—and thus also distorting—Romance forms; but as such a reaction could not take place in favour of a suppressed, or rather of a totally non-existing German form, the movement took a natural direction towards the discovery of an *ideal and purely human* form, such as could exclusively belong to no one nationality. The new and perfectly original activity of the two greatest German poets, Goethe and Schiller, unexampled in the history of art, is distinguished by the fact that they were the first who undertook the task of examining this problem of an ideal and purely human form of art in its most comprehensive signification; indeed, it may almost be said that the search after this form was the most essential part of their work. Rebelling against the restraint of that form which was still a law to the Romance nations, they came to consider it objectively, to see its inconveniences as well as its advantages, to return from it to the origin of all European form, that of the Greeks; to acquire, together with the necessary freedom, a full comprehension of the *antique*, and thence to rise to an *ideal* form of art, which being purely human and free from the restraint of narrow national custom, could develop such custom into a purely human one, subject only to the eternal laws of nature. The inferiority under which the Germanic nations, as contrasted with their Romance neighbours, had hitherto laboured, was thus turned into an advantage. Whilst the Frenchman, for instance, having before him a perfectly finished form, congruous in all its parts, obedient to its seemingly unchangeable laws, condemns himself to constant reproduction of this form, and therefore, in a higher sense, to a sort of stagnation in his inner productiveness, the German, fully acknowledging the advantages of such a position, would also recognise its considerable disadvantages; its shackles would not escape him, and the vista of an ideal form would extend itself before him wherein that which is imperishable in every form of art would appear freed from all fetters of what is only accidental and untrue. The immeasurable importance of such a form of art would necessarily consist in the fact that, being free from the restraint of a narrow nationality, it would become universally intelligible and accessible to all nations. If in regard to literature the attainment of this quality is hindered by the diversity of European languages, in music—the language understood by all men—we possess the great equalising power, which, resolving the language of intellectual conception into that of feeling, makes a universal communication of the innermost artistic intuitions possible, especially if this communication, by means of the plastic expression of a dramatic performance, could be raised to that distinctness which the art of painting has hitherto claimed as its exclusive privilege.

You have here before you a cursory plan of the work of art that presented itself to me more and more clearly as an *ideal*, the outlines of which I could not refrain from sketching theoretically at a time when my growing distaste for that "genre" of art which bears to my ideal conception the resemblance of an ape to a man, took such intense hold of me, that I felt obliged to retire from it into the deepest seclusion.

In order to make this crisis in my life intelligible to you, I must, without troubling you with biographical details, above all point out the singular contradiction which in our time a German musician experiences, who, with his heart filled with the spirit of Beethoven's symphony, has to turn to the composition of a modern opera of the kind which I have described to you as existing in Germany.

Notwithstanding a serious scientific education, I was from my earliest youth in constant and close contact with the stage. My youth was contemporaneous with the last years of Karl Maria von Weber, who periodically conducted his operas at Dresden, where I lived. From this master, whose melodies filled me with visionary earnestness, and whose personality attracted me with enthusiastic fascination, I received my first musical impressions. His death in a distant land filled my childish heart with sorrowful awe. Of Beethoven I knew nothing till I was told of his death, which shortly followed that of Weber; then I became acquainted with *his* music, as if drawn to him by the mysterious news of his decease. Strengthened by such earnest impressions, my inclination for music developed more and more. But it was not till later, after having become acquainted with classical antiquity, and having been thereby incited to some poetical attempts, that I came to study music seriously. I wished to compose the music for a tragedy I had written. It has been said of Rossini that he once asked his master whether, in order to compose an opera, it would be necessary for him to know counter-point? His master, referring the question to modern Italian opera, replied " Certainly not," whereupon Rossini gladly relinquished his contrapunctal studies. After my master had taught me the most difficult contrapunctal subtleties, he said to me, " You will probably never have occasion to write a fugue, but the fact of being able to write one will give you technical independence, and make everything else easy to you." After such schooling, I entered on the practical career of a conductor of music at a theatre, and began composing the music to " libretti " of my own.

Let this little biographical notice suffice. After what I have told you of the state of the opera in Germany, you will easily conceive the course of my further development. The singular gnawing pain I felt while conducting our ordinary operas, was often interrupted by an inexpressible enthusiastic pleasure, when, now and then, at the performance of nobler works, the astounding effect of some dramatic-musical combination impressed me deeply, fervently, and with an immediate vividness unapproached by any other art. It was the fact that such impressions, which in brilliant flashes showed me undreamt-of possibilities, returned again and again, that bound me to the theatre, no matter how profoundly disgusted I felt with the typical spirit of our operatic performances.

It was with especially lively impressions of this nature that I once heard an opera of Spontini's in Berlin, conducted by that master in person ; and, again, I felt for a time quite exalted and ennobled whilst studying Méhul's " Joseph " with a small opera company. When, about twenty years ago, I came to live in Paris, the performances at the " Grand Opéra," with their perfection of musical and plastic " mise en scène," could not fail to produce a dazzling and exciting effect upon me. In my earlier youth, I had already been intensely stimulated by the performances of a dramatic singer, which to me have remained unsurpassed—I mean Madame Schroeder-Devrient. Paris, too, and perhaps yourself became acquainted with this great artist. Her incomparable dramatic genius, the inimitable harmony and the individuality of her representations, which I witnessed with my own eyes and ears, fascinated and charmed me in a manner which gave a decided bias to my artistic direction. Having seen the possibility of such performances, and with a view towards them, I was enabled to set up a legitimate standard, not only as regards the musical-dramatic performance but also regarding the poetic-musical conception of a work to which I could scarcely continue to give the name of "*opera.*" It grieved me to see this artist under the necessity of stooping to the poorest operatic productions, in order to find scope for her talents ; and on the other hand again, I was filled with wonder at the warmth, the exquisitely fascinating charm with which she was capable of investing such a character as that of "Romeo" in Bellini's weak work ; at the same time I said to myself, what an incomparable work of art that might be, which would be perfectly worthy of such an artist's dramatic talents, or of the talents of a number of such artists.

The more these impressions strengthened my idea of what might be achieved in the "genre" opera, and the more feasible it seemed to me to realize it by leading the whole rich stream into which German music had swollen under Beethoven into the channel of this musical drama, the more disheartening and repulsive became my daily intercourse with the existing operatic business, so infinitely below the ideal I had conceived. Spare me the description of a growing disgust that became almost unbearable to an artist who, whilst seeing more and more clearly the possibility of realizing such incomparable perfection, saw himself confined within an impenetrable circle of daily occupations with a "genre" of art such as in its vulgar craftsman-like performance presented to him simply the contrary to his ideal conception. All my attempts at reform of operatic institutions, all proposals tending towards a realization of my ideal wishes by making *that* excellence, which appeared so rarely, the standard for *all* performances—all these efforts were in vain. I soon perceived clearly, what in reality is the aim and object of our modern theatre, and especially of the opera ; and it was this undeniable perception which so filled me with disgust and despair that, relinquishing all efforts at reform, I dropped my connection with that frivolous institution for good and all.

I had received the strongest inducement to account for the stagnation of our stage by the position it occupies in modern

society. I must admit that it was folly to imagine I could
entirely reverse the object of an institution which in its public
efficiency aims almost exclusively at providing diversion and
amusement for a population which loves pleasure because it is
bored, and at securing the pecuniary gain necessary to cover
the expenses of exhibitions calculated to serve such a purpose.
It was folly to think that I could substitute for this a wish
to raise people from the vulgar interests of daily life, to enable
them to comprehend and to adore the highest and the most
significantly beautiful that the human mind can grasp. I had
time to consider the causes which have reduced our stage to
the position it occupies in regard to our public life, and on the
other hand to take into account the foundations of those social
relations which would as necessarily produce the theatre I mean
as modern social relations produce our theatre. As I had found
in the rare appearances of artists of genius a basis for the character
of my dramatic-musical ideal, history also presented to me a type
for the ideal relation of the theatre, such as I imagined it, to
public life. This was the theatre of ancient Athens, which was
only opened on days of special festivity, when the enjoyment of
art was at the same time a religious celebration, in which the
most distinguished men of the State took part as poets or actors,
appearing like priests before the assembled populations of town
and country, who were filled with such high expectations of the
loftiness of the works to be performed, that Æschylus and
Sophocles could produce before them the profoundest of all
poems and be certain of their appreciation.

The reasons for the decline of this incomparable work of art,
which I looked for with deep pain, I soon discovered. My
attention was first drawn to the social causes of this decline and
they appeared to be identical with the causes of the decline of
the ancient State itself. Thence I endeavoured to deduce the
social principles of that political organization of the human race,
which correcting the imperfections of the antique State would be
able to found a condition of things, in which the relations
between art and public life, as it once existed in Athens, would

revive in a manner if possible even nobler and certainly more enduring. My thoughts on this subject I stated in a little pamphlet entitled " Die Kunst und die Revolution," my original intention, that of publishing it in a series of articles in a political French periodical, I relinquished on being assured that it was not a favourable time (1849) to gain the attention of a Parisian public for a subject of that description. At present it is I who judge it unbecoming to acquaint you more nearly with the contents of that pamphlet, and you will doubtless be thankful that I forbear to tax your patience with the attempt. Let it suffice that I have indicated therein the seemingly far removed meditations into which I was led whilst trying to find a basis for my artistic ideal—a basis which could—after all—be but an ideal reality.

For a comparatively longer time I then occupied myself with inquiring into the character of this deplorable dissolution of the great Greek work of art. The first thing that struck me was the remarkable fact, that those different branches of art which had previously been united in the perfect drama were now dissolved and separated. The mighty union by which it had been possible to make the most profound and exalted intentions of humanity perfectly intelligible to the people, had ceased to exist, and its component parts—the arts, as we call them—from inspiring public teachers now came to be but a pleasant pastime for individual lovers of art, so that while the people were publicly entertained with combats of gladiators and wild beasts, educated men occupied themselves with literature or painting, in private seclusion. It was especially important to perceive that the different arts in their separate and isolated cultivation, however their powers of expression might be increased and developed by brilliant genius, could never (without degenerating into unnaturalness and downright faultiness) aim in any way at replacing that all-powerful work of art, the production of which had only been possible to their combined efforts. With the aid of eminent art critics—Lessing, for instance, in his researches on the limits of painting and poetry—I arrived at the result that each separate branch of art developes itself to the full extent of its capabilities, and that, arrived at these limits, it cannot overstep them without incurring the risk of becoming incomprehensible and fantastical, nay, even absurd. At this point it seemed clear to me that each art once arrived at its limits demands to join itself to a sister art; and with my ideal in mind, it had a lively interest for me to trace these tendencies in each particular art; I seemed finally to be able to show it as existing most distinctly and strikingly in the relation between music and poetry, especially taking into consideration the great significance of modern music. Endeavouring thus to imagine a work of art of which all separate branches now unite each in its highest state of perfection, I arrived quite spontaneously at a clear conception of that ideal, which my mind had unconsciously formed for itself as a vague vision. As I was unable—remembering the thorough faulty relation of the stage to public life—to realize this ideal work of art in our own time, I called it " Kunstwerk der Zukunft,"—" Art work of the future." Under this title I published a pamphlet, in which I entered into a somewhat detailed exposition of the ideas just mentioned, and it is to this title, by the way, that we are indebted for that spectral invention a " Music of the Future," which haunts French and other reports on art and of which you will now easily perceive both the aim and the erroneous origin.

I will spare you the details of this pamphlet as well. I do not accord to it any other merit but what it may possess for those who would not consider it uninteresting to learn how and by what means a creating artist endeavoured to arrive, above all for his own behoof, at a solution of problems such as generally occupy only professional critics, but which can scarcely appear to them under the same peculiar aspect. Nor will I give you more than a general sketch of a third book on art which I published soon after the last-named, under the title of " Oper und Drama," as I cannot but feel that its fine-spun detailed exposition of my leading idea must possess a greater interest for myself than it can have for others, either now or in future. They were intimate meditations which, under the spur of the liveliest interest, I propounded partly in a polemical form. Their subject was a closer examination of the relation between poetry and music, and this time with special reference to the dramatic work of art. I felt it necessary, above all, to disprove the erroneous opinion of those who imagined that the ideal was, if not attained, at least immediately foreshadowed in the opera, properly so called. In Italy, and still more in France and Germany, the most eminent literary men have occupied themselves with this problem. The contest between the Gluckists and Piccinists was nothing but an intrinsically insoluable controversy as to the possibility of attaining an ideal drama in the opera; those who thought themselves justified in maintaining this thesis saw themselves, notwithstanding their apparent victories, kept in check by their adversaries, whenever these insisted upon the pre-eminence of music in opera by pointing out the fact that to *it* and not to poetry the latter owed its successes. Voltaire, who inclined theoretically towards the former opinion, when brought face to face with facts, was forced to his depressing saying, " *Ce qui est trop sot pour être dit, on le chante.*" In Germany the problem posed by Lessing was discussed by Schiller and Goethe with a decided inclination to expect the most favourable results from opera. Goethe, in striking contradiction to his own theory, involuntarily confirmed Voltaire's saying; for he himself wrote several libretti for operas wherein, placing himself on the level of the " genre," he deemed it advisable to be as trivial as possible, both in invention and in execution, so that we can only grieve to find these shallow pieces amongst his poems. The fact that this favourable opinion was so repeatedly entertained by the greatest minds without ever being realized. showed me on the one hand an apparently near possibility of reaching the very highest aim by a perfect union of music and poetry, and on the other hand, again, the fundamental faultiness of the opera—a faultiness which by reason of its very nature could not at first obtrude itself on a musician, and would necessarily also escape the notice of a literary poet. To a poet who was not himself a musician the opera appeared as a tightly-built scaffolding for musical forms, which from the very beginning prescribed the laws for inventing and executing the dramatic ground-work required of him. He had no power to alter anything in these forms; that was the province of the musician. The poet, who was called in as an auxiliary, disclosed involuntarily what these forms were worth by stooping to that triviality which Voltaire so justly ridiculed. It will be quite unnecessary to expose the poverty, the shallowness, nay, the utter absurdity of operatic libretti. Even in France the best attempts of this kind have consisted more in hiding the evil than in exterminating it. The real scaffolding of the opera has ever remained alien to the poet; he had simply to submit to it; and for this reason truly great poets, with rare and unfavourable exceptions, have never meddled with the opera. The question is now, how can it have been possible for a musician to give ideal significance to opera, when the poet in his practical contact with it was not even able to respond to the claims which we justly raise in regard to every decent play. How could this be effected by the musician, who is constantly occupied with the cultivation of purely musical forms, and who sees in the opera nothing but a field on which he can exercise his special musical talent? All that is contradictory and perverted in such claims on the musician I believe to have exposed clearly in the first part of my book " *Oper und Drama.*" In expressing my highest admiration of the exquisite beauties in the works of our great masters in music, I was not, when showing their weaknesses, obliged to detract from their fame, as I could prove the cause of these weaknesses to lie in the very faultiness of the " genre." But what I particularly wished to prove in this nevertheless unpleasant exposition was the fact that an ideal perfection of the opera, such as so many men of genius had dreamed of, could in the first instance only be attained by means of a total change in the character of *the poet's* participation in the work. Referring to the hopes and wishes, so frequently expressed by great poets, of attaining in the opera an ideal " genre," I came to believe that the poet's co-operation, so decisive in itself, would be perfectly spontaneous on his part and desired by him. I endeavoured to obtain a key to this aspiration, and thought to have found it in the desire (so natural to a poet, and which in him directs both conception and form) to employ the instrument of abstract ideas—language—in a manner which would take effect on the feelings. As this tendency is already predominant in the invention of poetical subject matter—and as only that picture of human life may be called poetical in which all motives, comprehensible to abstract reason only, disappear, so as to present themselves rather as motives of purely human feeling—this tendency is obviously the only one to determine the form and expression of poetical execution. In his language the poet tries to substitute the original sensuous signification of words for their abstract and conventional meaning, and, by rhythmical arrangement and the almost musical ornament of rhyme in the verse, to assure an effect to his phrase which will charm and captivate our feelings. This tendency, essential to the poet, conducts him finally to the limits of his art, where it comes into immediate contact with music. The most complete poetic work would therefore be that which in its ultimate perfection would resolve itself into *music*.

I was led to designate the " Mythos " as the ideal subject-matter for the poet—Mythos being that primitive poem of the people which we find at all times taken up and treated anew by great poets of cultivated periods ; for in it those conventional forms of human relations, explicable only to abstract reason, disappear almost entirely ; and in their place stands *that* which is for ever comprehensible, being purely human, but in that inimitable concrete form which gives to every genuine myth its strikingly individual character. The researches into this matter formed the subject of the second part of my book and brought me to the question as to which form would necessarily be the most perfect for the representation of this ideal practical material ?

In the third part I entered into an examination of technical possibilities as regards form, and came to the conclusion—*that nothing but the wonderfully rich development of Music in our time,*

C

totally unknown to earlier centuries, could have brought about the discovery of those possibilities.

I am too well aware of the ‚importance of this assertion not to regret that this place is not fit for a circumstantial exposition of my thesis. In the above-mentioned third part I believe to have done this in a satisfactory manner (for myself, at least), and if therefore I undertake to give you a slight sketch of my intention in regard to this subject, I beg you to receive in good faith the assurance that what may possibly appear paradoxical to you is more fully explained and supported by detailed proofs in the volume in question.

It is undeniable that since the Renaissance among the Christian nations of Europe, two special arts have received a new and complete development, such as they had not reached in classical antiquity—I mean painting and music. The wonderful ideal significance which painting gained as early as the first century of the Renaissance, is such an undoubted fact, and the characteristics of this significance have been so thoroughly explored, that I will only refer to the novelty of this phenomenon in the general history of art, and to the fact of its belonging entirely to *modern* art. In a higher, and I believe still more significant degree, we may make these assertions in regard to music. Harmony entirely unknown to antiquity, its incomparably rich development and extension by the aid of polyphony —these are the inventions and the most peculiar works of later centuries.

The Greeks knew music only as associated with dancing. The motion of the dance fixed the laws of its rhythm, as well as that of the poem sung by the dancer; these laws so distinctly determined both verse and melody, that Greek music (which almost invariably included poetry) can only be looked upon as dance expressing itself in words and sounds. These dance-melodies, which originally belonged to the worship of heathen gods, and which constituted the very essence of all ancient music, were also adopted by the early Christians for their gradually developing church music. This grave ceremony, which entirely excluded dancing as a worldly and Godless art, naturally also dropped the essential part of antique melody, namely, the exceedingly vivacious and varied rhythms, whereby the melody received that entirely unaccentuated character which it still retains in the plain chant of our churches. But by depriving this melody of its rhythmical mobility, they also took away its peculiar means of expression ; and we can thus convince ourselves, even to this day, of the uncommon poverty of expression in ancient melody when bereft of its ornament of rhythm, on imagining it without the harmony which at present supports it. The Christian spirit, in order to raise the expressive power of melody, invented polyphonic harmony on the basis of the four-part chord, which by its characteristic changes served henceforth as a motive of expression to the melody—an end which had formerly been attained by means of its rhythm. On hearing the incomparable masterpieces of Italian church music, we experience with ever returning emotion the effect of that wonderfully deep and hitherto unknown expression which the melodic phrase thereby attained. The different voices, which 'were originally only destined to make the harmonic chord heard in connection with the note of the melody, now received a free and progressive development, so that by aid of the so-called contrapunctal art each of these voices adapted to the melody proper (the *canto forms*) moved with independent expression ; thus producing, in the works of the most highly-gifted masters, church music of such wonderful. power, stirring the heart to its very depth, that the effects of no other art can be compared to it.

For the decline of this art in Italy and the simultaneous cultivation of operatic music on the part of the Italians, I can find no other appellation than a relapse into paganism. When, with the decline of the church, a worldly inclination became predominant in the Italians also in regard to the application of music, they solved the difficulty by restoring to the melody its original rhythmical properties, and thus applying it to song as it had formerly been applied to the dance. Modern verse was developed in unison with *Christian* melody. I shall refrain from pointing out the striking incongruities between it and the *dance* melody which was forced upon it. I only wish to call your attention to the fact that modern melody is almost entirely indifferent to the verse, and that its variation-like movement was in the end solely dictated by vocal virtuosi. But what chiefly induces me to call this cultivation of melody a retrogade step rather than a progress is the incontestable fact that it would not in the least utilize the important invention of Christian music—I mean harmony and polyphony—for its own purposes. Italian operatic melody has remained satisfied with a harmonic basis of such astounding poverty that it might exist without any accompaniment whatever. It has been content also in regard to the formation and connection of its parts with so mean a construction of phrases that cultivated musicians of the present time stand with sorrowful amazement before this scanty, almost childish form of art, the narrow limits of which condemn even the most gifted composer, if he deals with it, to a complete stability of form.

The same impulse towards secularization of church music reached a new and singular significance in Germany. The German masters too returned to the original rhythmical melody, as they found it living among the people, side by side with church music, in the form of the national dance tune. But instead of relinquishing the rich harmony of the former, German masters endeavoured, on the contrary, to develop harmony anew in connection with the lively rhythmical melody, and this in such a manner that rhythm and harmony contributed equally to the expression of the melody. Thus independent polyphony was not only retained but developed to a point where each of the voices, by means of contrapunctal art, took an independent part in the execution of the rhythmical melody, so that this melody was heard not only in the original *canto fermo*, but also distinctly in each of the accompanying voices. In church music, where the lyrical flow tends towards rhythmical melody, the wonderful and irrestible effect—an effect peculiar and possible to music alone—will be felt by all who are fortunate enough to hear a good performance of vocal compositions by Sebastian Bach—for instance, of his eight-part motet " Sing unto the Lord a new song," in which a lyrical stream of rhythmical melody seems to rush through a rolling sea of harmony.

But a still freer development, which rose to the most refined and varied expression, was reserved for the cultivation of rhythmical melody on the basis of Christian harmony in instrumental music. Leaving the orchestra for the present out of the question, let me draw your attention first to the extension in form of the original dance melody. By the development of the quartette of stringed instruments, polyphony worked a radical change in the treatment of the different orchestral parts, a change similar to that effected on the vocal parts of church music, and thus emancipated the orchestra from the inferior position it held at that time and still holds in Italian opera— a position in which it is used only for rhythmic and harmonic accompaniment. It is highly interesting—and at the same time the only way of elucidating the nature of all musical form— to observe how the German masters have all aimed at giving a richer and broader development to the simple dance melody, executed independently by instruments. This melody consisted originally of a short phrase of four bars, which were repeated twice or four times ; to give it a greater extension, and thereby to attain a broader form, in which the harmony might at the same time be displayed more richly, seems to have been the fundamental tendency of our masters. The peculiar form of the fugue applied to the dance melody furnished occasion for extending the duration of the piece by giving the melody to all voices alternately, by now shortening now prolonging it, by exhibiting it in the new light of harmonic modulations, and by means of contrapunctal secondary themes keeping up the interest in motion. Another proceeding consisted in stringing together several dance melodies, letting them change place in accordance with their expressive character, and connecting them by transitions in which the art of counterpoint proved particularly useful. That peculiar work of art, the symphony, was founded and developed on this simple basis. Haydn was the gifted master who first extended this form, and made it wonderfully expressive by the inexhaustible changes in the motives, as well as in their connections and transformations. Whilst the Italian operatic melody retained its poor construction, it had, nevertheless, when delivered by talented singers gifted with noble voices and warm feeling, received a sensuously beautiful colouring. This sweet euphony had been hitherto unknown to German masters, and was entirely wanting in their instrumental music. Mozart first realized the charm, and whilst giving to Italian opera the richer development of instrumental composition, he imparted on the other hand the sweetness of Italian singing to orchestral melody. Beethoven then took possession of the rich and promising inheritance left by Haydn and Mozart; he developed the symphonic work of art to such astonishing breadth of form, and filled this form with such marvelously various and entrancing wealth of melody, that we now stand• before his symphony as before a landmark of an entirely new period in the history of art; for in this symphony a phenomenon has arisen, the like of which has never existed in the art of any period or any nation.

In this symphony the instruments speak a language of which no one had hitherto any conception, inasmuch as the attention of the listener is held captive for a duration until this time unknown to all other arts; his feelings are moved by incredibly various nuances of purely musical expression, with a power disclosing in its changes an adherance to law, yet so free and bold that it must appear more powerful than all logic; not that it in the very least contains any laws of logic—on the contrary, rational thought, existing and moving in reasons and consequences, finds no hold whatever in it. Thus the symphony must appear to us like a revelation from another world; and in truth it discloses a connection of phenomena totally different from the usual logical connection, of which one thing is at all events quite undeniable—that this connection is felt with overpowering conviction, and that it directs our feelings with

an unerring certainty such as entirely confounds and disarms
all logical reasoning.

The metaphysical necessity for the discovery of this completely novel means of expression in our own times appears
to me to lie in the more and more conventional development
of modern speech. Examining the development. of modern
languages, we find to this day in the so-called roots of words
an origin which clearly shows that from the very first the
conception (Begriff) of any object was formed in a manner
coinciding almost entirely with the subjective feeling it called
forth, and the supposition that the first language of human
beings may have had a great resemblance to singing will,
perhaps, not appear ludicrous. Starting from a signification of
words which was at first entirely subjective (sinnlich subjectiv),
human language developed itself in a direction more and more
abstract in such wise that at last there remained only a
conventional signification of words, which deprived our feelings
of all direct participation in their sense, and their construction
and connection came to depend entirely on rules which had
to be learned. In necessary accordance with the moral development of men, conventions increased as regards manners and
speech, the laws of which were no longer intelligible to natural
feeling, but were enforced in educational maxims such as could
only be understood by reflection. Since modern European
languages, divided moreover into different branches, followed
their purely conventional development with a tendency more
and more obvious, music, on the other hand, retained a power
of expression such as the world had not yet known. It seems
that human sentiment, as if intensified by pressure of conventional civilization, had sought an outlet for asserting itself
according to its own laws of expression, by means of which
it would be able to render itself intelligible, quite independent
of the restraint of logical laws of thought. The astounding
popularity of music in our time, the ever-growing sympathy in
all grades of society with the production of the profoundest
kinds of music, the increasing zeal to make of musical culture

an important branch of education—all this, which is evident and undeniable, proves the correctness of the supposition that the modern development of music has met an innate desire of the human heart, and that music, however unintelligible its language may be according to the laws of logic, must necessarily possess a more convincing urgency to become intelligible than even those same laws themselves.

In the presence of this irrefragable cognition, there would be but two ways left open for the development of poesy (die Poesie): either an entire transplantation to the field of abstraction, a pure combination of conceptions and representations by explanation (Erklärung) of the logical laws of thought—and this poesy has done in the field of philosophy—or a close amalgamation with music, and in fact with that music whose wonderful power Beethoven's symphony has revealed to us.

Poesy will easily find the way to accomplish this, and will recognize its innermost want in the desire finally to resolve itself into music, as soon as it perceives in music again that want which can only be supplied by the poetic art. In order to explain this want, we first of all confirm the irradicable peculiarity of human perception which leads us to the discovery of the laws of causality, and by reason of which in presence of any impressive phenomenon we ask ourselves, "Why? Wherefore?" The hearing of a symphonic piece of music will not entirely silence this question—nay, more, not being able to answer it, the hearer finds his perception of causes confused in a manner not only calculated to disturb him, but also causing an entirely false judgment. The task of answering this unavoidable question, so as to silence and elude it completely, must be the poet's work. But only that poet can do this successfully who is fully aware of the tendency of music, and of its inexhaustible power of expression, and who therefore plans his poem so that it can penetrate to the finest fibres of the musical tissue, and that the conception expressed can resolve itself entirely into feeling. Hence the only form of poetry applicable to this purpose is that in which the poet no longer describes but presents his subject in a manner to strike and convince the senses, and this form is *the Drama.* The drama, at the moment of its representation on the stage, at once arouses in the spectator the intimate interest in an action which is so faithful an imitation of at least possible real life, that this interest itself raises the sympathetic sentiments of the spectator to a state of extasy where he forgets that fatal " Why ? " and thus stimulated, he willingly gives himself up to the guidance of those new laws according to which music becomes so wonderfully intelligible and, in a profound sense, gives the only correct answer to that " Why ? "

In the third part of the above-named book, I endeavoured to point out the technical laws occording to which this intimate amalgamation of music with poetry was to be effected in the drama. You will not expect me to repeat this explanation, for with the preceding outlines I have probably tired you as much as myself, and I perceive by my own fatigue that I am, quite against my wish, again approaching that mental state in which, years ago, I worked out those theoretical writings, and which affected my brain with such strangely morbid pressure that I called it an abnormal one—I have a lively dread of approaching it again.

I called it an abnormal state because I felt that, if I wished to render that perfectly distinct to my reflective perception which had become clear and certain to my artistic conception and production, I should have to treat it as a theoretical problem, and to this end had to make use of abstract meditation. But there is nothing more foreign and more painful to an artistic temperament than a process so opposed to his customary method of thought. He lacks the calmness which is necessary to the professed theorist; his passionate impatience prevents him from giving sufficient time to the careful treatment of style —he wants to give in each sentence a conception of the whole subject, and the doubts of the possibility of doing so urge him to constant repetition of the attempt, thus producing violent irritability, to which a theorist ought to be a stranger. At the same time he becomes conscious of all these faults and errors, the feeling of them adds to his trouble, and he at last hastily concludes his work with the sad conviction that he will after all probably be understood by those only who already share his own artistic views.

Thus my mental state resembled a struggle ; I tried to express theoretically that which, under the incongruity of my artisitic tendencies as opposed to the tendencies of our public art, especially of the opera, I could not state in a convincing manner by means of immediate artistic production. I felt a vivid desire to return from this painful state to the normal exercise of my artistic faculties. I designed and executed a dramatic project of such dimensions that by following only the exigencies. of my subject I intentionally set aside the possibility of introducing it into our operatic repertoire, such as it is. at the present time. It was only under the most extraordinary circumstances that I intended that this musical drama, which comprised a complete tetralogy, was to be publicly performed. This ideal possibility, in which I put the modern opera entirely out of sight, flattered my imagination and raised the tone of my mind to a height that, banishing all theoretical scruples, I was enabled by continued artistic production to fall back into my natural temperament, as if recovered from a long malady. The work to which I refer, and of which I have since also finished in great part the musical composition, is called " Der Ring des Nibelungen." If my present attempt of introducing to your notice a translation of some of my other operatic poems should gain your approval, I may perhaps be disposed to repeat the experiment with that cycle of dramas.

Whilst I rested, in complete retirement from the sufferings caused by my painful excursion into the land of speculative theory, and whilst I occupied myself with new artistic projects, my relations to the public took a direction on which I had least calculated.

My operas, one of which (" Lohengrin ") had never been performed at all, and the others only at the theatre in which

I had formerly occupied an active position, gradually found their way with increasing success into many of the German theatres, where they attained enduring and undeniable popularity. I was curiously surprised, but I had an opportunity of renewing certain observations I had often made during my former activity, and which, whilst I felt on the one hand a strong repugnance to the opera, on the other hand attracted me towards it by showing me exceptions and disclosing possibilities by the effect of some wonderfully fine performances, which, as I have already mentioned, made me conceive ideal projects. I was not present at any of those performances of my operas, and could therefore only draw my inferences in regard to their spirit from reports of intelligent friends and from their characteristic result with the public. The picture I deduced from my friends' reports was not calculated to inspire me with a more favourable opinion of the spirit of those performance than that which I had formed of our operatic performances in general. Thus on the whole confirmed in my pessimistic opinions, I now enjoyed the pessimist's advantage of deriving a more intense pleasure from the occasional unexpected appearances of what is good, nay excellent, whilst I had formerly as an optimist claimed the good and the excellent simply because it was possible, and so had become intolerant and ungrateful. Occasional excellent performances, of which I heard quite unexpectedly, filled me with new warmth and grateful recognition ; if the attainment of completely excellent artistic performances had hitherto appeared impossible to me under firmly established conditions, I now recognized the possibility of their being exceptionally attainable.

But what struck me still more forcibly was the extraordinarily warm impression my operas had produced upon the public, even when executed in so inferior a manner as sometimes actually to distort them. When I consider the dislike and hostility of those critics to whom my former publications on art were an abomination, and who obstinately believed my operas—which had been written at an earlier period—to have been composed with full intent according to those theories—when I take into consideration how these critics expressed themselves against my operas—I cannot but see a highly important and encouraging sign in the fact that the public expressed unequivocal approbation of my works and their tendency. When German critics once exclaimed, "Turn away from Rossini's seductive syren songs, shut your ear to his shallow melodies," the public disregarded the critical cry, and continued to hear them with pleasure. This was easy to understand; but in my case the critics incessantly warned the public not to spend money upon that which could not possibly give them pleasure; for what they alone sought in operas—melodies, melodies, melodies—did not exist in mine; there was nothing in them but wearisome *recitatives* and the most unintelligible conglommerate of musical cacophony; in short, "Music of the Future!"

Imagine the effect it had upon me to receive not only irrefutable proofs that my operas had attained real popularity with the whole German public, but also individual acknowledgments of a complete conversion from people who, after finding pleasure only in the most lascivious tendencies of the opera and the ballet, had hitherto turned a disgusted and contemptuous ear to any suggestion of a more serious tendency in the dramatic-musical art. I have not unfrequently met with such converts, and I will tell you what encouraging and consoling conclusions I have thought myself justified in drawing from the fact.

Evidently the question was not one concerning the greater or lesser strength of my talents, since even hostile critics did not pronounce themselves against that, but rather against the tendency which I followed, choosing to ascribe my success to the fact that my talent was better than my tendency. Quite untouched by their possibly flattering recognition of my capacities, I could only rejoice that I had started from a correct instinct when I hoped to find in the mutual penetration (Durchdringung) of music and poetry that work of art which would, at the moment of scenic performance, make an irresistible impression, and this in such a manner that all voluntary reflection would have to resolve itself into purely human feeling. The fact

that this effect had been attained, in spite of considerable
weakness in the performance, the perfect correctness of which
must, on the other hand, be of so much importance to me—
this fact has inclined me to still more hopeful views of the all-
powerful efficiency of music, upon which point I will finally
try to explain myself to you.

I can only hope to express myself clearly upon this difficult
but exceedingly important point by confining myself to *form*.
In my theoretical works I had tried to determine substance
together with form ; as in theory my exposition could only be
abstract, not concrete, I exposed myself to misinterpretations,
not to say unintelligibility. I would therefore, as I have already
observed, here avoid a return to such a proceeding at any
risk. Nevertheless, I perceive the difficulty of speaking about a
form without in any way pointing out its substance. As I have
confessed to you at the onset, I should not have ventured to
attempt giving you a valid explanation of my theoretical proceeding if you had not at the same time requested me to
place a translation of some of my operatic poems before you.

I must, however, beg your indulgence for offering you a
prose translation of these poems. The endless difficulties I had
in procuring a translation in verse of " Tannhäuser," which is
soon to be introduced to the Parisian public, have proved that
such translations demand an amount of time which could not
in this instance be devoted to my other pieces. I must therefore
give up the hope of your being in any way impressed by the
poetical form of these pieces, and content myself with showing
you the character of the " sujet " and its dramatical treatment
and tendency, in order thereby to point out the share which
the spirit of music had in its conception and construction. For
this purpose I hope you will find the translation sufficient, for
it has no other claim but that of rendering the original text with
the greatest possible accuracy.

The first three of these poems, " Der fliegende Holländer,"
" Tannhäuser," and " Lohengrin," had already been written and
composed before I wrote my theoretical pamphlets, and had,

with the exception of "Lohengrin," also been performed. In them I might, therefore, if their "sujets" allowed me to do so efficiently, point out to you the progress of the artistic development to the point where I felt induced to give myself a theoretical account of my proceeding. I only mention this, however, in order to show you how greatly people are mistaken when they assume that I consciously constructed these three works by abstract rules. Let me assure you that even my most daring conclusions in regard to the musical-dramatic form, such as I deemed it possible to attain, presented themselves to me through the fact that I was at the same time occupied with the plan for my extensive "Nibelungen" drama, of which I had already written a part, and which I was forming in my mind in a manner to cause my theory to be nothing but the abstract expression of the process of artistic production which was growing within me. My particular system, if you choose to call it so, is therefore only applicable to these first three poems with considerable limitation.

But the case is quite different with the last of these poems, Tristan und Isolde." This I conceived and completed after already having finished the greater part of the musical composition of " Die Nibelungen." What induced me to pause in this extensive work was the desire to produce something which, by reason of its less ambitious proportions, that would render it better calculated for scenic performance, would enable me to hear once more some production of my own—a wish which my encouraging experiences in regard to the performances of older works in Germany seemed to place within my grasp. This work I will most willingly submit to the severest test based on my theoretical principle; not that I constructed it after my system—for I entirely forgot all theory—but because I here moved freely, independent of all theoretical scruples, in such a manner that, even during my labour, I became conscious how far I had gone beyond my system. Believe me, there can be no greater pleasure than an artist's perfect abandonment while composing — such as I felt it whilst working at " Tristan."

Perhaps it was owing solely to the fact of my having gained strength by reflection during the preceding period—much as my master asserted that he had strengthened me with difficult contrapunctal discipline—not with a view towards the writing of fugues, but towards that which can only be acquired by severe study—self-dependence and technical certainty!

Permit me briefly to mention an opera which preceded the "Fliegende Holländer"—"Rienzi," a work full of youthful fire, which gained my first success in Germany, and which continues to be performed not only at the theatre of Dresden, where I produced it first, but, together with the rest of my operas, at many other German theatres. I do not attach any special importance to this work, which was conceived and executed under the influence of my earliest impressions received from Spontini's heroic operas and from the glittering "genre" of the Parisian Grand Opéra, as represented by Auber, Meyerbeer, and Halévy—I do not, I say, attach any importance to it at present, because it does not embody any essential phase of my later artistic views, and because I have no intention of representing myself to you as a successful composer of operas, but rather in order to enlighten you in regard to the problematical direction of my tendencies. I completed "Rienzi" during my first sojourn in Paris—I had the splendid "Grand Opéra" before me, and was presumptuous enough to flatter myself with the hope of seeing my opera performed on that stage. Should this wish of my youth still be realized, you will agree with me that the decrees of Fate are indeed wonderful, placing as they do so long an interval between a wish and its accomplishment, and allowing such totally different experiences to accumulate.

This five-act opera, constructed on the very largest scale, was immediately followed by the "Fliegende Holländer," which I originally intended to be performed in one act. You perceive that the splendour of the Parisian ideal had already commenced to wane in my eyes, and that I began to draw the laws for the form of my conceptions from a different source than the sea of recognized publicity which lay before me. The substance of my state of feeling (Stimmung) is clearly shown in the poem; what poetical value may be accorded to it I do not know, but this I do know, that even whilst writing the poem I felt very differently than whilst writing the libretto of " Rienzi," where I was simply thinking of an opera-text which would enable me to display the principal forms of " Grand Opéra," such as introductions, finales, choruses, arias, duets, trios, etc. etc., with all possible splendour.

In this work, as well as in all the following, I turned, in the choice of my subject, once for all from the field of history to that of popular tradition. I refrain from stating the inner tendencies which led me to this decision, and will only point out the influence which this choice of subjects had upon the structure of the poetical, and especially the musical form. All details necessary for the description and representation of historical and conventional things—all delineations of a distinct and distant historical epoch, such as modern writers of historical novels and plays treat so circumstantially—all this I could pass over. Thus the necessity of treating the poem, and most especially the *music*, in a manner totally foreign to their nature, was entirely obviated. The legend, to whatever time or nation it may belong, has this advantage, that it assumes nothing of such a time and such a nation but what is purely human, and renders this in a form, peculiar to itself, of great pregnancy, and therefore at once perfectly intelligible. A ballad, a popular refrain, is sufficient to give us instantly a clear impression of this character. The traditionary colouring in which a purely human action is represented to us has, moreover, the genuine advantage of considerably facilitating the task which I assigned to the poet—namely, that of presenting and appeasing the question " Why? " The characteristic scene as well as the legendary tone immediately serve to throw the mind into that dreamy state in which it soon arrives at a perfect clairvoyance, perceives a new connection in the phenomena of the world— a connection of which the waking perception can never become aware, and thus constantly recurs to the " Why? " as if desirous of conquering the terror of what is incomprehensible in the world—the world which has now become so perfectly clear and intelligible. You will comprehend easily how music is destined finally to achieve and complete the charm by which this state of *clairevoyance* is brought about.

As regards the poetical development, a legendary subject possesses this one essential advantage that, whilst the simple progress of the external action is so obviously intelligible that it requires no explanation, it admits, on the other hand, of the greater part of the poem being devoted to the inner motives of the action—motives which by reason of our own sympathetic interest in them, can alone finally prove to us the necessity of this action.

On perusing the poems which I have laid before you, you will easily perceive that I only gradually became conscious of the advantage which I have been pointing out, and only by degrees have learned to make use of. The increased bulk of each poem will prove this. You will soon see that the embarrassment which at first prevented me from giving a broader development to the poem, principally arose from the fact that I was still too much under the influence of the traditional forms of operatic music, which had hitherto made a poem that did not admit of numerous verbal repetitions nearly impossible. In "Der fliegende Holländer," my general aim in the first instance consisted only in preserving the action in its simplest traits, in excluding all unnecessary detail, such as the intrigue of every-day life, and in place thereof to carry out those traits which threw the proper light on the characteristic colour of the legendary subject-matter—a colour which appeared to coincide with the peculiar inner motives of action—in such a manner as to turn that very colour into action.

In "Tannhäuser" you will find the action to be developed from its inner motives with a much greater force. The final catastrophe emerges without the least constraint from the lyrical-poetical contest where no other power than that of the innermost sentiments brings it about in such wise that even its form remains purely lyrical.

The interest in "Lohengrin" rests entirely upon a process in the heart of Elsa, which touches all the secrets of the soul—the duration of a charm that spreads, with convincing truth, a wonderful happiness over all surroundings, depends entirely upon her refraining from the question "Whence?"—the question bursts like a cry of despair from the deep anguish of a woman's heart, and the charm has vanished. You divine how strangely this tragical "Whence?" coincides with the theoretical "Why?" of which I have been speaking!

I too, as I have already said, had felt irresistibly drawn towards these questions "Why?" and "Whence?" which had for a long time obscured the charm of my art for me. But the time of my penitence taught me to conquer this question—all doubt had flown when I began "Tristan." With perfect confidence I allowed myself to become absorbed in the workings of the soul, and unhesitatingly out of this most intimate centre of the world I shaped their external form. A single glance at the bulk of this poem will show you that I ventured to apply the same detailed distinctness which the poet of a historical subject must give to the external connection of his action to the detriment of a clear representation of the inner motives, to the latter only. Life and Death, the whole signification and existence of the external world, in this work depends entirely on the emotions of the soul. The whole affecting action becomes prominent only because it is demanded by the innermost sentiment and comes to light as it has been prepared in the depths of the soul.

Perhaps you will think that in this poem I went too much into detail, and, whilst you may concede such a privilege to the poet, you may wonder how he could venture to entrust all these finer details to the musical composer. In this case you would be deceived by the same prejudice which induced me, even in the conception of the "Fliegende Holländer," to give but a very general outline of my intentions in the poem which was only to serve as a scaffolding for absolute musical execution. But to this allow me to reply at once, that whilst *there* the verses were written so that, by means of frequent repetition of words and phrases, they might be extended to a breadth nece ssary to the melody, I have admitted no repettiion of words in the musical execution of " Tristan," and that in " Tristan " the entire extent of the music is, as it were, prescribed in the tissue of words and verses—that is to say, that the musical melody is already contained in the poem.

Should I have been successful throughout, it may perhaps be sufficient for you to allow that a much more intimate amalgamation between ihe poem and the music will be attained by this procedure than by the old one ; and if I might at the same time hope that you could see more merit in the poetical execution of " Tristan " than there can possibly be found in my former works, you would from this circumstance have to draw the conclusion that the fact of the musical form being already traced in the poem must have been advantageous to the poetical workmanship.   If, therefore, the complete prefiguration of the musical form in the poem is capable of giving a particular value to it (which quite corresponds with the desire of the poet), the question only remains whether by this proceeding the musical form of the melody is not prejudiced by being deprived of its freedom in movement as well as development?

To this question let me as a musician reply with a deep conviction of the correctness of my assertion, that by this proceeding the melody and its form acquire an inexhaustible wealth, of which, without it, no one could form any conception. With the theoretical proofs of this proposition let me conclude this communication. I will endeavour to keep only the musical form—the melody—in view.

In the reiterated cries of our superficial musical amateurs for Melody ! Melody ! I find the confirmation that they derive their idea of melody from musical works in which, side by side with melody, there is a sustained tunelessness serving as background for the melody they talk of.   In Italy the opera served to bring people together who wished to be amused of an evening ; a part of their amusement consisted in the music to be heard on the stage, which was now and then listened to when the talk flagged : during the conversation and the visits from box to box the music continued, with the object which characterizes it at state dinners —to encourage by its noise a timid conversation. Music performed for such ends and for such conversation fills the main part of an Italian operatic score, whilst the music that is properly listened to forms, perhaps, the twelfth part of it. An Italian opera must contain at least *one* air that people care to listen to; if it is to be successful, interesting music must interrupt the conversation at least six times; but a composer who is able to fix the attention of his audience for a whole dozen of times is praised as an inexhaustible melodic genius. How, then, can a public be blamed which finds itself suddenly in presence of a work claiming attention from beginning to end, which sees itself disturbed in all its habits during musical performances, and cannot possibly accept as identical with its beloved melody that which may, by great good fortune, appear as a refinement of the musical noise such as in its naïve application used to facilitate the most agreeable conversation, whilst it now urges a pretension of being listened to? Such a public would surely call for its six or twelve melodies, if only to obtain in the interval an opportunity and an excuse for the real object of the operatic evening— conversation.

In truth, that which a strangely narrow vision takes for wealth must appear as poverty to the educated mind. The noisy demands founded upon this error can be forgiven to the public at large, but not to the art-critic. Let me try, therefore, as far as may be possible to explain both the error and its cause.

Let us settle, first of all, that *the only form of music is melody*, that without melody music is not conceivable, and that music and melody are entirely inseparable. That a particular piece of music has no melody therefore means, in a higher sense, only that its author has not achieved the organization of a form such as is capable of distinctly determinating our feeling. This simply proves the composer to lack talent, shows the want of originality which obliged him to manufacture his piece out of familiar musical phrases, such as, by reason of their familiarity, leave the ear unimpressed. But when delivered by the uneducated lover of opera and in the presence of real music, this verdict indicates that only a narrow form of melody can be meant, which, as we have partly seen already, belongs to the infancy of musical art—for that reason, the preference accorded appears indeed childish. The question here is not so much one of melody, but of the first narrow form it assumes in the dance-tune.

In truth I do not wish to express myself depreciatingly upon this first origin of melodic form. I believe I have shown it to be the basis of the finished and complete form of Beethoven's symphony, and thus we are indebted to it for something perfectly astounding. But we must bear one thing in mind ; in the Italian opera this form is still in its primitive and undeveloped state, whilst in the symphony it has arrived at an extension and perfection, by reason of which it stands, as compared to the former, in the relation of the flower-crowned plant to the shoot. I therefore entirely accept the signification of the original form of melody—the form of dance-tune—and true to the principle that every form, however highly developed, must bear evident traces of its origin, if it is not to become unintelligible, I trace this dance-form in Beethoven's symphony, nay, I would have this symphony, considered as a melodic complex, looked upon simply as the *idealized dance-form.*

Let us first observe that this form extends over all parts of the symphony, being in this respect the reverse of the Italian opera, inasmuch as there the melody stands entirely alone, and the intervals between the single melodies are filled up with a species of music which we are bound to designate as absolutely unmelodious, because in it the music has not yet lost its character of mere noise.

Even in the symphonic movements of Beethoven's immediate predecessors, we still find these suspicious voids between the principal melodies ; if *Haydn* generally succeeded in giving to these intervals a very interesting significance, *Mozart*, who came far nearer to the Italian conception of melodic form, has frequently, nay, almost usually, fallen back upon that trivial structure of phrases in the light of which his symphonic movements not unfrequently appear akin to so-called dinner-music, namely, that kind of music which in the intervals of pleasant melodies furnishes also a pleasant noise for the promoting of conversation. I, at least, always feel as though I were listening to the clatter of dishes on a princely table set to music, when I hear the ever-recurring and noisy semi-cadences of Mozart's symphonies. Beethoven's procedure, so peculiar and full of the highest genius, consisted, on the contrary, in getting entirely rid of these unpleasant intermediate periods, and of giving the connections between the principal melodies a fully melodious character.

A closer examination of this procedure, although exceedingly interesting, would here lead us too far. Yet I cannot refrain from drawing your attention especially to the construction of the first movements of Beethoven's symphonies. Here we find the dance-melody proper, dismembered into its minutest particles, each of which, frequently consisting of only two sounds, always appears, now in rhythmical, now in harmonic character, interesting and expressive. These parts continually unite, forming new combinations, now flowing streamlike in regular sequence, now dividing as in a whirl—always fascinating by so plastic a movement that the listener cannot for a moment escape its impression, but feels convinced by the intense interest it awakens that each harmonic note, nay, each rhythmic pause, has a melodic significance. Thus the entirely novel result of this proceeding consists in the extension of the melody by the rich development of all its component motives into a large, long-sustained piece of music, which is nothing but a single strictly coherent melody

It is a remarkable fact that this procedure, which had been attained on the field of instrumental music, was in some measure applied by German masters to mixed choral and orchestral music, but hitherto never sufficiently to the opera. Beethoven has in his great Mass treated chorus and orchestra almost with the same freedom as in his symphonies. He could make use of this symphonic treatment because in the words of the service, known to all the world and of little more than symbolical significance, he was provided with a form which he could divide and connect somewhat in the same manner as the dance-melody. But it was impossible that an intelligent musician could think of treating the words of a dramatic poem in this fashion, because these cannot be content with a symbolical significance only, but must have a distinct logical sequence. But this again applied only to libretti calculated for the traditionary forms of the opera; on the other hand, there remained the possibility of attaining a poetical counterpart to the symphonic form in a dramatic poem which, completely filling this rich form, would also respond to the innermost laws of the drama.

The problem here touched, most difficult to treat theoretically, may perhaps be made clear if I use a metaphorical form.

I have called the symphony the realized ideal of melodic dance-form. Beethoven's symphony really contains in the parts called "Menuetto" or "Scherzo" an entire primitive dance-music, to which one could dance if need be. The composer would seem to have been compelled by an instinctive desire to touch once in the progress of his work upon its immediate real basis, feeling as it were with his feet for the ground that is to bear him. In the other movements he recedes more and more from the possibility of having a real dance performed to his melody, unless it were so ideal a dance that it would stand to the primitive dance in the same relation as the symphony stands to the original dance-tune. So we find here a kind of hesitation on the part of the composer not to overstep certain limits of musical expression, especially not to pitch the passionate tragical tendency too high, because he would thereby awaken emotions and expectations which must arouse in the hearer that troublesome question "Why?" which question the musician would not be able to answer satisfactorily.

The dance that would perfectly correspond to this music—this ideal form of dance—is in truth the *dramatic action.* Its relation to the primitive dance is really that of the symphony to the simple dance-melody. The original people's dance, too, expresses an action, mostly the mutual wooing of lovers; such simple action, taken in its richest imaginative development as the expression of the innermost emotions of the soul, results in what we call the dramatic action. You will spare me, I trust, the attempt to prove that our ballet does not sufficiently represent such an action. The ballet is own brother to the opera, starting from the same faulty basis, for which reason we love to see both go hand in hand—as if for mutual covering of their shortcomings.

It is, therefore, not a *programme* which wakens that objectionable question "Why?" more than it removes it, but only the dramatic action embodied on the stage, which can fully express the significance of symphonic music.

In regard to this assertion, of which I have already given the reasons, I need only point out here the animating and expanding effect which a perfectly adequate poem can have upon the melodic form. The poet who has perfectly mastered the inexhaustible power of expression of the symphonic melody, will feel induced to meet the finest and most delicate "nuances" of this melody, which by one single harmonic turn is capable of the most touching changes of expression; no longer fettered by the narrow form of operatic melody, he will cease to furnish only a dry and empty canvas; he will, on the contrary, learn a secret as yet unsolved by the musician himself—namely, that the melodic form is still capable of infinitely richer development than musicians had hitherto believed possible in the symphony; and filled by a presentiment of this development, he will trace the details of his poetical conception with unfettered freedom.

Where the symphonist still timidly returned to the original dance-form and never ventured to depart entirely, even for expression's sake, from the boundaries which connected him with this form—there the poet will call to him: "Throw yourself fearlessly into the sea of music—hand in hand with me you can never lose the connection with what is most intelligible to all men, for with my aid you always stand on the ground of dramatic action, and this action, at the moment of scenic representation, is the most immediately intelligible of all poems.

Spread your melody boldly, so that it may flow through the whole work like an uninterrupted stream; with it reveal all that I pass over in silence, because *you* only can reveal it, and, silently, I will reveal all, leading you by the hand."

Indeed, the greatness of the poet is mostly to be measured by what he leaves untold, so that we may silently tell ourselves the inexpressible—the musician it is who gives voice to that which has remained untold, and the infallible form of his sounding silence is *infinite melody*.

Evidently the symphonist will not be able to construct this melody without his peculiar instrument—this is the orchestra. I need not emphasize the fact that he will use this instrument in a manner totally different from that of the Italian operatic composer, in whose hands it is little more than a monstrous guitar for the accompaniment of arias.

To the drama of my conception the orchestra will bear a relation similar to that of the Greek chorus to the dramatic action. This chorus was ever present, before its eyes the motives of the action in course of representation developed themselves, it tried to penetrate these motives and to draw from them the conclusions upon which to found its opinion on the action. Only this participation was throughout more of a reflective nature, and the chorus remained a stranger to the action as well as to its motives. The orchestra of the modern symphonist, on the contrary, will be so intimately joined to the motives of the action, that, on the one hand, as embodied harmony it renders the distinct expression of melody possible, whilst, on the other hand, it keeps the melody in the necessary uninterrupted flow, and thus always displays the motives of the dramatic action with most convincing impressiveness to our feelings. If we have to consider that form of art as the ideal one, which can be understood without reflection, and by which the artist's conception communicates itself in the purest manner to the feelings; and if we agree to recognize, under the above-named suppositions, this ideal form of art in the *musical drama*, the symphonist's orchestra is the wonderful instrument for the only possible representation of this form. That in the presence of the orchestra and its importance the chorus, which in the opera has appeared on the stage, entirely loses the signification of the antique Greek chorus, is evident; it can henceforth only be considered in the light of an active person, and where it is not required as such it will in future appear superfluous and disturbing to us, since its ideal participation in the action has been entirely transferred to the orchestra, and is by the latter proclaimed in an ever present but never disturbing manner.

I must once more have recourse to metaphor in order finally to point out to you the characteristic of the large melody, which comprises the whole dramatic-musical piece, and to this end refer to the impression it must produce. The infinitely rich and ramified details of it are to reveal themselves not only to the connoisseur, but also to the most naïve layman as soon as he may be sufficiently collected to receive the impression. Its effect upon him is to be at first similar to that of a fine forest of a summer night on a solitary visitor, who has just left the town-noise behind him; the peculiarity of this impression upon the soul, which an experienced reader can develop for himself in all its effects, consists in the perception of the ever-growing eloquence of silence. As far as the work of art is concerned, it may in general be deemed sufficient to have produced this fundamental impression, and by its means imperceptibly to guide the hearer and to dispose him towards a higher intention; he thus unconsciously receives in himself the higher tendency. Just as a visitor to the woods, over-come by the total impression, rests to collect his thoughts, and then, gradually straining the powers of his soul, distinguishes more and more clearly, as it were with new senses, the multi-tudinous forest voices. He hears songs such as he believes never to have heard before—multiplied they gain in strange power, louder and louder they grow; and however many voices or separate songs he hears, the overpowering clear swelling sound appears as the one great forest-melody, which at first disposed him to devotion, like unto the deep blue sky of night which at

other times attracted his eye, until, being completely absorbed
in the night, he beheld more distinctly the countless hosts of
stars. This melody will never cease to haunt him; but repeat
or hum it he cannot; to hear it again he must return to the
woods on a summer night. Would it not be folly if he were
to catch a sweet woodbird, so as to train it at home to whistle
a fragment of that great forest-melody? And what would he
hear if he succeeded?—which melody?

What an immense number of technical details I have left
untouched in the preceding superficial sketch, which is nevertheless already too long, you will readily conceive when you
consider that these details are in their nature of inexhaustible
variety even in theoretical exposition. In order to make myself
understood in regard to all the particulars of melodic form, as
I wish to see it conceived—clearly to define its relations to the
ordinary operatic melody and the possibility of its extension
as regards periodic construction as well as harmony—to do this,
I should simply have to relapse into my former fruitless attempt.
I therefore content myself with presenting only the most general
tendencies to the reader, for in truth we are, even in this sketch,
already approaching that point where finally only the work of
art itself can give full explanation.

You would be mistaken if you thought that with this last
observation I intended an allusion to the impending representation of "Tannhäuser." You are acquainted with my score
of "Tristan," and although I do not think of representing it
as a model of the ideal, you will nevertheless allow that from
"Tannhäuser" to "Tristan" I have taken a wider step than
I had done from my first stand-point—that of the modern opera
—to "Tannhäuser." Whoever, therefore, looks upon this letter
as a preparation for the performance of "Tannhäuser," would,
in some respects, have conceived very erroneous expectations.

Should I have the good fortune to see "Tannhäuser" favourably
received by the Parisian public, I feel sure that I shall owe this
success in great part to its very evident relationship with some of
the works of my predecessors, amongst whom I would call your

attention particularly to Weber. But permit me briefly to point out to you in what respect my opera can be distinguished from its precursors.

It is clear that everything which I have here pointed out as the strictest consequence of an ideal proceeding, has at all times also lain within reach of our great masters. Nor did I myself arrive at these conclusions in regard to the possibility of an ideal work of art by purely abstract reflection, but most assuredly by means of my observation of the works of our masters. The great *Gluck* still was checked by the narrowness and stiffness of operatic forms as he found them, standing without connection side by side, and which he certainly did not expand on principle. His successors already knew how to enlarge and combine these forms in such a manner that they proved quite sufficient for the attainment of the highest aims, especially when an important dramatic situation gave them a chance. To acknowledge the great, the powerful, and the beautiful in point of dramatical-musical conception in many of the works of our revered masters, to support this by example seems utterly unnecessary; certainly no one is readier to acknowledge this with joyful praise than I am; for I do not even disguise from myself that in the weaker works of frivolous composers I have sometimes come upon special effects which astonished me, and which gave proof of that wonderful power of music, which I have already spoken of, and which by means of the firm precision of melodic expression lifts even the least gifted singer so high above the level of his personal performances that he produces an effect which must remain unattainable to the most talented and experienced artist of the simple spoken drama. But what from the first especially saddened and annoyed me was the fact that I never found all these unequalled advantages of dramatic music developed in the opera to an equable and pure style which would embrace all the parts. I found in the most important and significant works, side by side with the noblest and most perfect efforts, the most incomprehensibly senseless things—flat conventionality of expression, nay, even frivolity.

If we find the objectionable juxtaposition of absolute recitatives and absolute aria, so detrimental to a perfect style, retained nearly everywhere, and if we thereby see the musical stream (by reason of a faulty poem) constantly interrupted and impeded, we also find that in their finest scenes our great masters have frequently quite surmounted this evil. The recitativo itself has there already received a rhythmic and melodic significance, and it unites itself insensibly with the broader structure of melody proper. After once having realized the great effect of this proceeding, how painfully it grates upon us, when we suddenly hear the vulgar chord which announces the *recitativo secco;* but with the same suddenness the full orchestra then strikes up the inevitable *ritornello* that ushers in the aria, the same *ritornello* which has elsewhere, under the treatment of the same master, been so significantly employed in the connection and transition; of whose eloquent beauty we suddenly became aware when it acted as an interesting comment on the dramatic situation. But what if a piece, that is simply calculated to pander to the lowest taste in art, follows immediately upon one of those beautiful blossoms? Or still worse, when a touchingly beautiful phrase suddenly ends with the stereotyped cadenza with the usual runs and the inevitable forced note just before the close, with which the singer all of a sudden leaves the person whom he or she was addressing, and steps to the footlights, thus giving the signal for applause to the "claque"?

It is true that the latter inconsistencies do not occur in the works of our great masters, but rather with those composers on hearing whose works we are amazed that they should have produced the exceptional beauties of which I have been speaking. The very serious aspect of the facts in question is, however, this—that after all the noble and perfect achievements of great masters with which they come so near to a perfectly pure style in opera, these relapses could still occur, nay, that what was unnatural should have gained ground more than ever.

The chief reason for this is undeniably a humiliating regard for the character of the *peculiar opera-going* public, which with inferior artists always has the greatest weight. Did not Weber himself—that pure, noble, and sensitive mind, whom the consequences of his method sometimes frightened—did not even he invest his wife with the "rights of the gallery," as he expressed it, so that she might, in the spirit of the gallery, raise objections to his conceptions, such as would induce him here and there to be less strict in regard to his style and to make a few concessions?

These "concessions," which my first beloved model, Weber, felt bound to make for the operatic public, you will not, as I think I may flatter myself, find in "Tannhäuser;" and as to the form of the work, it is perhaps *that* which distinguishes it from those of my predecessors. I required no special courage for this; for on the impressions which excellent things in the "genre" of opera have hitherto produced upon the public, I have founded an opinion of this public which has led me to adopt the most favourable views. The artist who addresses his work of art not to the abstract but to the intuitive perception, presents it intentionally not to the connoisseur but to the public. Only as much as this public may be penetrated with a critical spirit, and may have lost the ingenuousness of purely human perception (Anschauung), need the artist feel uneasy. It is just because of its manifold concessions that the opera, as it has hitherto existed, appears to me calculated to confuse the public, for, not knowing what to expect, people involuntarily begin to reflect when reflection is least wanted, and their natural hesitation is aggravated by the senseless talk of those who assume a connoisseurship. If we observe the infinitely greater decision with which the public expresses its opiniou on a simple play, how nothing in the world will induce it to declare an absurd action to be sensible, an ill-fitting speech to be apt, or a false emphasis to be true, we gain in this fact a safe support upon which the opera can be brought into relations with the public.

A second point which distinguishes "Tannhauser" from the opera proper is the *dramatical poem* upon which it is founded.

Without intending to attach any value to it as a poetical production, I still think myself justified in calling your attention to the fact that, although based upon legendary and partly supernatural matter, it contains a consistent dramatical development, in the conception and execution of which no concessions have been made to the common-place requirements of an operatic libretto. My intention, above all, is to attach the interest of the public to the dramatic action in such a manner that it is never obliged to lose sight of it, but that, on the contrary, all musical ornament appears only as a means of representation. Thus it was the rejection of all concessions in the subject-matter that enabled me to reject those concessions also for the musical execution, and in these facts you will find that which constitutes my "innovation;" and most certainly not in an absolute musical arbitrariness, which people have thought fit to impute to me, as a tendency inherent in the "music of the future."

Permit me to tell you, in conclusion, that notwithstanding the great difficulty of obtaining a perfectly corresponding poetical translation of "Tannhäuser," I confidently place my work before the Parisian public. That to which a few years ago I could not have made up my mind without great anxiety—this I now approach with the confidence of one who sees in his proceeding not so much a speculation as a matter of interest to his heart. This change of feeling I owe more particularly to the frequent encouragement I have met with since I last established myself in Paris; amongst these pleasant experiences was one which quickly filled me with joyful surprise. You, dear friend, permitted me to approach you as one who was already well acquainted with me. Without having witnessed a performance of one of my operas in Germany, you had already, as you gave me to understand, for some time past, carefully read my scores. The acquaintance thus acquired with my works had awakened in you a wish to see them performed in Paris, nay, had brought you to believe that you might promise yourself a favourable and not unimportant impression upon the Parisian public from these performances. As you thereby helped to give me confidence in my undertaking, you will bear me no ill-will if I have fatigued you with these perhaps too detailed explanations, and will ascribe my zeal in meeting your request to my great desire of giving to the friends of my art a clearer insight into those ideas for which I could not well expect any one to look in my former writings on art.

RICHARD WAGNER.

Paris, September, 1860.

THE WORKS OF RICHARD WAGNER,

PUBLISHED AND SOLD BY

SCHOTT & CO., REGENT STREET, LONDON, W.

Die Meistersinger von Nürnberg.

Oper in 3 Akten.

	£	s.	d.
Vollständige Orchester-Partitur (full score) ... ... nett	6	0	0

VOCAL.

	£	s.	d.
Vollständiger Clavier-Auszug (Vocal score) von CARL TAUSIG nett	1	8	0
Lyrische Stücke aus der Oper *Die Meistersinger von Nürnberg.*			
No. 1. POGNER'S ANREDE. Nun hört, und versteht mich recht.—B.	0	3	0
,, 2. WALTHER VOR DER MEISTERZUNFT. Am stillen Herd in Winterszeit—T.	0	2	6
,, 3. WALTHER'S WERBEGESANG. Fanget an ; So rief der Lenz—T.	0	2	6
,, 4. MONOLOG VON SACHS. Was duftet doch der Flieder so mild—B.	0	2	6
,, 5. SACHSEN'S SCHUSTERLIED. Jerum ! Jerum ! Halla hallohe !—B.	0	3	0
,, 6. JOHANNISLIED DAVID'S. Am Jordan St. Johannes stand—T.	0	1	6
,, 7. MONOLOG VON SACHS. Wahn ! Wahn, Ueberall Wahn !—B.	0	2	6
,, 8. WALTHER'S TRAUMLIED. Morgenlich leuchtend in rosigem Schein—T....	0	2	6
,, 8 *bis.* The same for Baritone...	0	2	6
,, 9. CHOR DER SCHUSTER. Sankt Krispin,lobet ihn !—T.B.	0	2	6
,, 10. CHOR DER SCHNEIDER. AlsNürnberg belagert war—T.B.	0	2	0
,, 11. QUINTETT. Selig, wie die Sonne—2 S. 2 T. & B.	0	2	6
,, 11 *bis.* EVA'S TAUFSPRUCH. Selig wie die Sonne—S. ...	0	1	6
,, 12. GRUSS AN SACHS. Wach'auf, es nahet gen den Tag— S. A. T. & B.	0	1	6
,, 12 *bis.* The same for Soprano Solo	0	1	6
,, 13. WALTHER'S PREISLIED. Morgenlich leuchtend in rosigem Schein—T....	0	2	6
,, 13 *bis.* The same for Baritone...	0	2	6
,, 14. SACHSEN'S SCHLUSSLIED. Verachtet mir die Meister nicht—B.	0	2	6

PIANOFORTE SOLOS.

	£	s.	d.
Vollständiger Clavier-Auszug zu 2 Händen, ohne Text (the complete Opera as a Pianoforte Solo) ... ... nett	0	16	0
Vorspiel (Overture)	0	3	6
Id. Concertparaphrase, übertragen von H. von BÜLOW	0	5	0
Einleitung zum 3 Akt (Introduction to the third act)...	0	2	0
BEYER, F. Répertoire des jeunes Pianistes. Petites fantaisies instructives sur des motifs d'Opéras favoris. Op. 36, No. 109. *Die Meistersinger von Nürnberg*	0	3	0
———Bouquet de Mélodies. Op. 42, No. 88. *Die Meister- singer von Nürnberg*	0	4	0
BRUNNER, C. T. 3 kleine Tonstücke über Motife aus der Oper *Die Meistersinger von Nürnberg.* Op. 490.			
No. 1. Am stillen Herd	0	3	0
,, 2. Am Jordan	0	3	0
,, 3. Sei'euch vertraut	0	3	0

Die Meistersinger von Nürnberg (continued).

		£	s.	d.
BÜLOW, H. VON. *Die Meistersinger von Nürnberg*. Versammlung der Meistersingerzunft. Bruchstück aus Akt 1. (Concert-paraphrase)		o	3	o
————— *Dis Meistersinger von Nürnberg*. Paraphrase des Quintetts aus dem 3 Akte		o	3	o
CRAMER, H. *Die Meistersinger von Nürnberg*. Potpourri No. 172		o	3	6
————— Marsch über Motife aus der Oper *Die Meistersinger von Nürnberg*		o	2	6
————— Tanz der Lehrbuben aus der Oper *Die Meistersinger von Nürnberg*. Transcription		o	3	o
JAELL, A. 2 Transcriptionen aus der Oper *Die Meistersinger von Nürnberg*. Op. 137.				
·No. 1. Walther's Werbegesang (1 Akt)		o	3	6
,, 2. Walther's Preislied (3 Akt)		o	4	o
————— Walther vor der Meisterzunft. "Am stilen Herd" aus der Oper *Die Meistersinger von Nürnberg*. Transcription. Op. 148		o	4	o
LASSEN, E. *Die Meisersinger von Nürnberg* (Les Maîtres-chanteurs de Nuremberg). Transcriptions de salon. 2 Hefte.				
Heft 1. Aufzug der Zünfte. Walther's Gesang. Beckmesser's Ständchen. Walther's Preislied		o	3	6
,, 2. Choral. Sachsen's Monolog. Finale des 1 Akts. Tanz der Lehrbuben. Sachsen's Schusterlied. Chor der Lehrbuben. Marsch der Meistersinger		o	4	6
LEITERT, G.' *Die Meistersinger von Nürnberg*. Transcrip. Op. 26		o	2	6
LISZT, F. "Am stillen Herd." Lied aus der Oper *Die Meistersinger von Nürnberg*. Transcription		o	5	o
RAFF, J. Reminiscenzen aus der Oper *Die Meistersinger von Nürnberg*. 4 Hefte.				
Heft 1. Choral. Chor der Lehrbuben. Walther's Gesang. Finale		o	4	o
,, 2. Scene zwischen Walther und Eva. Sachsen's Schusterlied. Strassentumult. Finale		o	4	o
,, 3. Volkslied vom heiligen Johannes. Ensemblestück. Tanz		o	3	6
,, 4. Die selige Morgentraum-Deutweise. Aufzug der Zünfte. Marsch der Meistersinger		o	4	6

PIANOFORTE DUETS.

Volständiger Clavier-Auszug zu 4 Händen, ohne Text (the complete Opera as a Pianoforte Duet) ... ... nett		1	4	o
Vorspiel (Overture) eingerichtet von A. HORN		o	5	o
Id. ,, ,, C. TAUSIG		o	6	o
Einleitung zum 3 Akt (Introduction to the third act)...		o	2	o
BEYER, F. Revue mélodique. Collection de petites fantaisies instructives à quatre mains sur des motifs d'Opéras favoris. Op. 112, No. 56. *Die Meistersinger von Nürnberg*		o	4	o
BÜLOW, H. VON. *Die Meistersinger von Nürnberg*. Versammlung der Meistersingerzunft. Bruchstück aus Akt 1. Paraphrase		o	4	6
CRAMER. H. *Die Meistersinger von Nürnberg*. Potpourri. No. 82		o	5	o
————— Marsch über Motife aus der Oper *Die Meistersinger von Nürnberg*		o	4	o

TWO PIANOFORTES.

Vorspiel (Overture) für 2 Pianofortes zu 8 Händen eingerichtet von C. DEPROSSE		o	9	o

HARMONIUM.

KASTNER, E. Paraphrase über Motife der Oper *Die Meistersinger von Nürnberg*, für Harmonium. Op. 5		o	3	o

Die Meistersinger von Nürnberg (continued).

VIOLIN AND VIOLONCELLO.

		£	s.	d.
GOLTERMANN, G. Walther's Lied aus der Oper *Die Meister-singer von Nürnberg*, für Violine mit Pianofortebegleitung ...		o	2	6
Id. für Violoncell mit Pianofortebegleitung		o	2	6
GREGOIR, J., UND LEONARD, H. Duo für Pianoforte und Violine über Motife der Oper *Die Meistersinger von Nürnberg.* No. 35		o	7	o
WICKEDE, FR., VON. Lyrische Stücke aus R. WAGNER's Musik-Dramen, übertragen für Violoncell mit Pianofortebegleitung.				
No. 1. Walther vor der Meisterzunft		o	4	o
,, 2. Walther's Preislied		o	3	6

ORCHESTRA.

		£	s.	d.
Vorspiel (Overture) für grosses Orchester. Partitur (full score) ...		o	12	o
Id. Stimmen (Orchestral parts)		o	18	o
STASNY, L. Potpourri für kleines Orchester		o	16	o
Die Meistersinger von Nürnberg, Textbuch (Libretto)		o	1	6

Der Ring des Nibelungen.

TRILOGIE.

VORSPIEL

DAS RHEINGOLD.

Musikalisches Drama in 4 Scenen.

		£	s.	d.
Vollständige Orchester-Partitur (full score) ... ... nett		4	o	o
Vollständiger Clavier-Auszug (Vocal score) eingerichtet von K. KLINDWORTH ... ... nett		o	16	o
Id. id. ohne Text zu 2 Händen (the complete opera as a Pianoforte Solo) ... ... nett		o	10	o
Vorspiel (Overture) für das Pianoforte zu 2 Händen		o	2	6
BEYER, F. Répertoire des jeunes Pianistes. Petites fantaisies instructives sur des motifs d'Opéras favoris. Op. 36, No. 110.				
Das Rheingold		o	3	o
————— Revue mélodique. Collection de petites fantaisies instructives à quatre mains sur des motifs d'Opéras favoris. Op. 112, No. 57. *Das Rheingold* (Duet)		o	4	o
CRAMER, H. *Das Rheingold.* Potpourri pour Piano. No. 175		o	3	6
HEINTZ, A. Angereihte Perlen aus dem *Rheingold*. Für Pianoforte		o	4	6
JAELL, A. *Das Rheingold.* Erste-Scene. Transcription. Für Pianoforte. Op. 120		o	5	o
GREGOIR, J., UND LEONARD, H. *Das Rheingold*. Duo pour Piano et Violon. No. 38		o	7	o
Das Rheingold, Textbuch (Libretto)		o	1	o

ERSTER THEIL

DIE WALKÜRE.

Musikalisches Drama in 3 Aufzügen.

Vollständige Orchester-Partitur (full score). In the press.

VOCAL.

		£	s.	d.
Vollständiger Clavier-Auszug (Vocal score) eingerichtet von K. KLINDWORTH ... ... nett		1	o	o
No. 1. Ein Schwert verhiess mir der Vater—T.		o	2	6
,, 2. Siegmund's Liebesgesang. Winterstürme wichen dem Wonnemond—T.		o	2	6
,, 3. Siegmund ! sieh auf mich—S. T.		o	6	o
,, 4. War es so schmählich, was ich verbrach—S. B. ...		o	8	o

Der Ring des Nibelungen (continued).

PIANOFORTE SOLOS.

	£	s.	d.
Vollständiger Clavier-Auszug, zu 2 Händen, ohne Text (the complete Opera as a Pianoforte Solo) ... ... nett	0	14	0
Vorspiel (Overture)	0	2	6
Der Ritt der Walküren	0	4	0
Wotan's Abschied und Feuerzauber	0	4	0
BEYER, F. Répertoire des jeunes Pianistes. Petites fantaisies instructives sur des motifs d'Operas favoris. Op. 36, No.			
111. Die Walküre	0	3	0
CRAMER, H. Die Walküre. Potpaurri. No. 177	0	4	0
GREGOIR, J. Die Walküre. Transcription	0	3	6
HEINTZ, A. Angereihte Perlen aus der Walküre. In 3 Heften.			
Heft 1. Erster Aufzug	0	4	6
,, 2. Zweiter Aufzug	0	4	6
,, 3. Dritter Aufzug	0	6	0
JAELL, A. Die Walküre. Wotan's Absched und Feuerzauber. Transcription. Op. 121	0	6	0
———— Liebeslied aus der Walküre. Improvisation. Op. 149	0	5	0
LEITERT, G. Die Walküre. Souvenir. Op. 27	0	3	0
TAUSIG, C. Siegmund's Liebesgesang aus der Walküre. frei übertragen	0	3	6
———— Der Ritt der Walküren frei übertragen	0	5	0

PIANOFORTE DUETS.

	£	s.	d.
BEYER, F. Revue mélodique. Collection de petites fantaisies instructives à quatre mains sur des motifs d'Opéras favoris. Op. 112. No. 58. Die Walküre	0	3	6
CRAMER, H. Die Walküre. Potpourri. No. 89	0	5	0
TAUSIG, C. Der Ritt der Walküren, frei übertragen	0	7	0

HARMONIUM.

	£	s.	d.
KASTNER, E. Die Walküre. Reminiscenzen für Harmonium...	0	3	6

VIOLIN AND VIOLONCELLO.

	£	s.	d.
GREGOIR, J., UND LEONARD, H. Duo für Pianoforte und Violine, über Motife der Oper Die Walküre. No. 34 ...	0	7	0
WICKEDE, FR. VON. Lyrische Stücke aus R. WAGNER's Musik-Dramen, übertragen für Violoncell mit Pianofortebegleitung. No. 3. Siegmund's Liebeslied	0	3	6
Die Walküre, Textbuch (Libretto)	0	1	0

ZWEITER THEIL

SIEGFRIED.

Musikalisches Drama in 3 Aufzügen.

	£	s.	d.
Volständige Orchester-Partitur (full score). In the press.			
Volständiger Clavier-Auszug (Vocal score) eingerichtet von K. KLINDWORTH ... ... nett	1	4	0
Id. Id. ohne Text zu 2 Händen (the complete Opera as a Pianoforte Solo) ... ... nett	0	16	0
Vorspiel (Overture) für das Pianoforte zu 2 Händen	0	2	6
BEYER, F. Répertoire des jeunes Pianistes. Petites fantaisies instructives sur des motifs d'Opéras favoris. Op. 36. No.			
112. Siegfried	0	3	0
———— Revue mélodique. Collection de petites fantaisies instructives à quatre mains sur des motifs d'Opéras favoris. Op. 112, No. 59. Siegfried (Duet)	0	4	0
CRAMER, H. Siegfried. Potpourri pour Piano. No. 180 ...	0	3	6
———— Id. Potpourri à quatre mains. No. 91 (Duet)	0	5	0
JAELL, A. Id. Transcription für Pianoforte. Op. 146 ...	0	5	0
———— Id. Etude-Transcription pour Pianoforte. Op. 147	0	4	0
Siegfried, Textbuch (Libretto)	0	1	6

DRITTER THEIL
GÖTTERDÄMMERUNG.
Musikalisches Drama in 3 Aufzügen.
(In the Press.)

Tannhäuser und der Sängerkreig auf Wartburg.

Romantiche Oper in 3 Akten.

VOCAL.		£	s.	d.
The complete Opera (Vocal score), with German words, 4to	nett	1	4	0
Id. id. with French words, 8vo	,,	0	15	0
Id. id. ,, Italian words, ,, ...	,,	1	0	0
Romance de l'Etoile du soir, " O mein holder Abendstern "	...	0	3	0

PIANOFORTE SOLOS.

	£	s.	d.
BEYER, F. Répertoire des jeunes Pianistes. Petites fantaisies instructives sur des motifs d'Opéras favoris. Op. 36, No. 52. *Tannhäuser*	0	3	0
———— Bouquet de Mélodies. Op. 42, No. 57. *Tannhäuser*	0	4	0
CRAMER, H. *Tannhäuser.* Potpourri. No. 110	0	3	6
GORIA, A. Id. Fantaisie-Caprice de Concert. Op. 97	0	5	0
JAELL, A. Id. Gebet der Elisabeth. Transcription. Op. 48	0	3	6
———— Id. Pilgerchor. Transcription. Op. 60. No. 1	0	2	6
———— Id. Lied an den Abendstern. Transcription. Op. 60, No. 2	0	2	6
NEUSTEDT, CH. *Tannhäuser.* Fantaisie-Transcription. Op. 88	0	3	6
SCHMEER, G. Marsch über Motife aus dem *Tannhäuser*	0	1	6
Marche du *Tannhäuser* (Einzug der Gäste auf Wartburg)	0	2	6
Einzug der Gäste auf Wartburg, eingerichtet von F. LISZT...	0	4	0
Ouverture	0	4	0
Id. Concertparaphrase, eingerichtet von F. LISZT ...	0	10	6

PIANOFORTE DUETS.

	£	s.	d.
BEYER, F. Revue mélodique. Collection de petites fantaisies instructives sur des motifs d'Opéras favoris. Op. 112, No. 25. *Tannhäuser*...	0	4	0
BEYER, F. Episodes musicales. Collection de Duos élégantes sur des airs favoris. Op. 136, No. 2. Marche de l'Opéra *Tannhäuser*	0	3	6
CRAMER, H. *Tannhäuser.* Potpourri. No. 40 ...	0	5	0
WOLFF, E. Grand Duo sur des motifs de l'Opéra *Tannhäuser.* Op. 239 ... ...:	0	7	0
Einzug der Gäste auf Wartburg. Marsch und Chor...	0	4	0
Ouverture	0	6	0

VIOLIN AND VIOLONCELLO.

	£	s.	d.
BÜLOW, H., VON, ET SINGER, E. Fantaisie concertante, pour Piano et Violon, sur des motifs de l'Opéra *Tannhäuser* ...	0	12	0
GREGOIR, J., ET LEONARD, H. Grand Duo brillant, pour Piano et Violon, sur des motifs de l'Opéra *Tannhäuser*. No. 26	0	8	0
———— ET SERVAIS, F. Duo brillant, pour Piano et Violoncelle, sur des motifs de l'Opéra *Tannhäuser*. No. 10	0	8	0
LEONARD, H. L'Etoile du soir. Romance de l'Opéra *Tannhäuser*, transcrite pour Violon avec accompagnement de Piano ...	0	3	6

HARMONIUM.

	£	s.	d.
DRINNENBERG, F. Souvenir de l'Opéra *Tannhäuser*. Pour Orgue-Mélodium avec accompagnement de Piano	0	4	0

CLARIONET.

	£	s.	d.
GREGOIR, J-, ET BLAES, J. Grand Duo brillant, pour Piano et Clarinette, sur des motifs de l'Opéra *Tannhäuser* (d'après Gregoir et Léonard)	0	8	0

Lohengrin.

Romantische Oper in 3 Akten.   £ s. d,
Volständige Orchester-Partitur (full score)   ...   ., nett 7 0 0

VOCAL.

The complete Opera (Vocal score), with German words, 4to   nett 1 4 0
  Id.   id.   with French words, 8vo   ...   ...   ·   ,,   0 15 0
  Id.   id.   with Italian words, 8vo   ...   ...   ,,   1 0 0

PIANOFORTE SOLOS.

BEYER, F.   Répertoire des jeunes Pianistes.   Petites fantaisies
  instructives sur des motifs d'Opéra favoris.   Op. 36, No. 53.
  Lohingrin 0 3 0
————— Bouquet de Mélodies.   Op. 42, No. 61.   Lohengrin... 0 4 0
CRAMER, H.   Lohengrin.   Potpourri.   No. 113...   ...   ... 0 3 6
GREGOIR, J.   Lohengrin.   Illustration 0 4 6
JAELL, A.   Lohengrin.   Gebet.   Transcription.   Op. 47   ... 0 2 0
LEYBACH, J.   Lohengrin.   Fantaisie.   Op. 125...   ...   ... 0 5 0
LISZT, Fr.   Transcriptionen aus Lohengrin.
  Elsa's Brautzug zum Münster 0 2 0
  Festspiel und Brautlied 0 6 0
  Elsa's Traum und Lohengrin's Verweis an Elsa 0 3 0
NEUSTEDT, Ch. · Lohengrin.   Fantaisie-Transcription.   Op. 89 0 4 0
Vorspiel (Overture) 0 1 6
Einleitung zum 3 Akt (Introduction to the third act)...   ...   ... 0 1 6

PIANOFORTE DUETS.

BEYER, F.   Revue mélodique.   Collection de petites fantaisies
  instructives sur des motifs d'Operas favoris.   Op. 112, No. 32.
  Lohengrin 0 4 0
CRAMER, H.   Lohengrin.   Potpourri.   No. 41 ...   . 0 5 0
WOLFF, E,   Grand Duo brillant sur des motifs de l'Opéra
  Lohengrin.   Op. 238   ...   . 0 7 0
Vorspiel (Overture) 0 1 6
Einleitung zum 3 Akt (Introduction to the third act)...   ...   ... 0 2· 0

VIOLIN AND VIOLONCELLO.

GREGOIR, J., und LEONARD, H.   Duo für Pianoforte und
  Violine über Motife der Oper Lohengrin.   No. 37   ... 0 7 0
————— et SERVAIS, F.   Grand Duo pour Piano et
  Violoncelle sur des motifs de l'Opéra Lohengrin.   No. 13 ... 0 8 0
SINGELLE, J. B.   Lohengrin.   Fantaisie pour Violon avec ac-
  compagnement de Piano.   Op. 123   ...   . 0 7 0
WICHTL, G.   Petits morceaux de salon pour Violon avec ac-
  compagnement de Piano.   Op. 75, No. 3.   Lohengrin   ... 0 5 0

FLUTE.

BRICCIALDI, G.   Lohengrin.   Fantaisie pour Flûte avec ac-
  compagnement de Piano,   Op. 129   ...   . 0 7 0

Der Fliegende Holländer.

(LE VAISSEAU-FANTÔME)
Romantische Oper in 3 Aufzügen.

VOCAL.

The complete Opera (Vocal score), with German words (Der
  Fliegende Holländer.. 4to   ...   . nett 1 4 0
  Id. id. with French words (Le Vaisseau Fantôme). 8vo, ,,   0 15 0.
  Id, id. with Italian words (Il Vascello-Fantasma). 8vo, ,,   0 15 0

Der Fliegende Holländer (continued).

PIANOFORTE SOLOS.

		£	s.	d.
BEYER, F.　Répertoire des Jeunes Pianistes.　Petites fantaisies instructives sur des motifs d'Opéras favoris.　Op. 36, No. 37.　Der Fliegende Holländer (Le Vaisseau-Fantôme)		o	3	o
BEYER, F.　Bouquet de Mélodies.　Op. 42, No. 66.　Der Fliegende Holländer (Le Vaisseau-Fantôme)		o	4	o
CRAMER, H.　Der Fliegende Holländer (Le Vaisseau-Fantôme).　Potpourrj.　No. 137		o	3	6
———— Chœur des matelots Norvegiens.　Op. 116, No. 2		o	3	6
JAELL, A.　Der Fliegende Holländer.　Spinnerlied (La Fileuse).　Transcription.　Op. 143		o	4	o
———— Id.　Ballade.　Transcription.　Op. 144 ...		o	3	6
LISZT, FR.　Spinnerlied aus dem Der Fliegenden Holländer ...		o	5	o
NEUSTEDT, CH.　Le Vaisseau-Fantôme.　Fantaisie-Transcription.　Op. 90		o	3	6
Ouverture		o	4	o

PIANOFORTE DUETS.

		£	s.	d.
BEYER, F.　Revue mélodique.　Collection de petites fantaisies instructives sur des motifs d'Opéras favoris.　Op. 112, No. 14.　Der Fliegende Holländer (Le Vaisseau-Fantôme) ...		o	4	o
CRAMER, H.　Der Fliegende Holländer (Le Vaisseau-Fantôme).　Potpourri.　No. 62		o	5	o
WOLFF, E.　Grand Duo sur des motifs de l'Opéra Le Vaisseau-Fantôme.　Op. 243		o	7	o
Ouverture		o	7	o

VIOLIN AND VIOLONCELLO.

		£	s.	d.
GREGOIR, J., ET LEONARD, H.　Le Vaisssau-Fantôme (Der Fliegende Holländer.　Duo pour Piano et Violon.　No. 46		o	8	o
———— ET SERVAIS, F., FILS.　Le Vaisseau-Fantôme.　Duo pour Piano et Violoncelle.　No. 24		o	8	o

Reinzi.

DER LETZTE DER TRIBUNEN.

Grosse tragische Oper in 5 Akten.

VOCAL.

		£	s.	d.
The complete Opera (Vocal score), with German words, 2 vols., 4to. ... ... nett		2	8	o
Id.　id.　with French words, 8vo ... ... ,,		1	o	o
Id.　id.　with Italian words 8vo ... ... ,,		1	o	o

PIANOFORTE SOLOS.

		£	s.	d.
BEYER, F.　Répertoire des jeunes Pianistes.　Petites fantaisies instructives sur des motifs d'Opéras favoris.　Op. 36, No. 97.　Rienzi		o	3	o
———— Bouquet de Mélodies.　Op. 42, No. 37.　Rienzi ...		o	4	o
CRAMER, H.　Rienzi.　Potpourri.　No. 146		o	3	6
JAELL, A.　3 improvisationen aus Rienzi.				
Gebet " Allmächtiger Vater blick' herab."　Op. 99 ...		o	3	6
Arie. "In seiner Blüthe bleicht mein Leben."　Op. 100 ...		o	3	o
Terzett. "Adriano du."　Op. 101		o	3	o
KETTERER, E.　Rienzi.　Fantaisie-Transcription.　Op. 107 ...		o	4	6
KÜRGER, W.　Chœur des Messagers de Paix, de Rienzi.				
Op. 160.　Edition de Concert		o	5	o
Op. 160 bis.　,,　Salon		o	4	o
NEUSTEDT, CH.　Rienzi.　Fantaisie-Transcription.　Op. 87 ...		o	3	6
Ouverture		o	4	o
Friedensmarsch aus Rienzi		o	2	6

Rienzi (continued).

PIANOFORTE DUETS.

	£	s.	d
BEYER, F. Revue mélodique. Collection de petites fantaisies instructives sur des motifs d'Opéras favoris. Op. 112, No. 44. *Rienzi*	0	4	0
CRAMER, H. *Rienzi*. Potpourri. Op. 88	0	5	0
WOLFF, E. Grand Duo sur des motifs de l'Opéra *Rienzi* ...	0	7	0
Ouverture	0	7	0

VIOLIN AND VIOLONCELLO.

	£	s.	d
GREGOIR, J., UND LEONARD, H. Duo für Piano ·und Violine über Motife der Oper *Rienzi*. No, 36	0	7	0
———— ET SERVAIS, J., FILS. *Rienzi*. Duo pour Piano et Violoncelle. No. 23	0	8	0

Tristan und Isolde.

Handlung in 3 Aufzügen.

	£	s.	d
Vollständige Orchester-Partitur (full score) ... ... nett	7	0	0
Vollständiger Clavier-Auszug (Vocal score), 4to ... ... „	1	8	0
CRAMER, H. *Tristan und Isolde*. Potpourri pour Piano. No. 158	0	3	6
JAELL, A. 3 Stücke für Pianoforte aus *Tristan und Isolde*.			
Transcription. Op. 112	0	3	0
Illustration. Op. 113	0	4	6
Paraphrase. Op. 114	0	3	0
Vorspiel (Overture) für Pianoforte	0	2	0

Huldigungs Marsch für Ludwig II. König von Bayern.

	£	s.	d
Für grosses Orchester. Partitur (full score)	0	8	0
Stimmen (Orchestral Parts)	1	1	0
Für Pianoforte eingerichtet (as a Pianoforte Solo)	0	3	6
„ „ von H. von BÜLOW	0	3	6
„ zu 4 Händen eingerichtet von H. von BÜLOW (as a Pianoforte Duet)	0	4	6
Für 2 Pianofortes zu 8 Händen eingerichtet	0	8	0

Fünf Gedichte. für Eine Frauenstimme.

	£	s.	d			£	s.	d
No. 1. Der Engel	0	2	0	No. 4. Schmerzen		0	1	6
„ 2. Stehe still	0	2	0	„ 5. Traume		0	2	0
„ 3. Im Triebhaus	0	2	0	Complete in 1 book		0	7	0

	£	s.	d
LEONARD, H. Fünf Gedichte, für Violine und Pianoforte übertragen	0	7	0

Die Beiden Grenadiere.

(LES DEUX GRENADIERS.)
Gedicht von Heine.

	£	s.	d
Für eine Singstimme mit Pianofortebegleitung (German and French words)	0	3	0

3 Chansons.

	£	s.	d
No. 1. *Dors, mon enfant.*			
En Fa	0	3	0
En Ré-*bémol*	0	3	6
No. 2. *Mignonne.*			
En Mi	0	3	0
En Ut	0	3	0
No. 3. *Attente.*			
En Fa	0	3	0
En Ut	0	3	0

Der Tannenbaum.

BALLADE.

	£	s.	d
Für eine Singstimme mit Pianofortebegleitung	0	3	0

.

Music and Books published by Travis & Emery Music Bookshop:

Anon.: Hymnarium Sarisburiense, cum Rubricis et Notis Musicis.
Anon.: Säcularfeier des Geburtstages von Ludwig van Beethoven
Agricola, Johann Friedrich from Tosi: Anleitung zur Singkunst.
Bach, C.P.E.: edited W. Emery: Nekrolog or Obituary Notice of J.S. Bach.
Bateson, Naomi Judith: Alcock of Salisbury
Bathe, William: A Briefe Introduction to the Skill of Song
Bax, Arnold: Symphony #5, Arranged for Piano Four Hands by Walter Emery
Burney, Charles: The Present State of Music in France and Italy
Burney, Charles: The Present State of Music in Germany, The Netherlands …
Burney, Charles: An Account of the Musical Performances ... Handel
Burney, Karl: Nachricht von Georg Friedrich Handel's Lebensumstanden.
Burns, Robert: The Caledonian Musical Museum ..The Best Scotch Songs. (1810)
Cobbett, W.W.: Cobbett's Cyclopedic Survey of Chamber Music. (2 vols.)
Corrette, Michel: Le Maitre de Clavecin
Crimp, Bryan: Dear Mr. Rosenthal … Dear Mr. Gaisberg …
Crimp, Bryan: Solo: The Biography of Solomon
Crotch, William: Substance of Several Courses of Lectures on Music
d'Indy, Vincent: Beethoven: Biographie Critique
d'Indy, Vincent: Beethoven: A Critical Biography
d'Indy, Vincent: César Franck (in French)
Fischhof, Joseph: Versuch einer Geschichte des Clavierbaues. (Faksimile 1853).
Frescobaldi, Girolamo: D'Arie Musicali per Cantarsi. Primo & Secondo Libro.
Geminiani, Francesco: The Art of Playing the Violin.
Handel; Purcell; Boyce; Geene et al: Calliope or English Harmony: Volume First.
Häuser: Musikalisches Lexikon. 2 vols in one.
Hawkins, John: A General History of the Science and Practice of Music (5 vols.)
Herbert-Caesari, Edgar: The Science and Sensations of Vocal Tone
Herbert-Caesari, Edgar: Vocal Truth
Hopkins and Rimboult: The Organ. Its History and Construction.
Hunt, John: - see separate list of discographies at the end of these titles
Isaacs, Lewis: Hänsel and Gretel. A Guide to Humperdinck's Opera.
Isaacs, Lewis: Königskinder (Royal Children) A Guide to Humperdinck's Opera.
Kastner: Manuel Général de Musique Militaire
Lacassagne, M. l'Abbé Joseph : Traité Général des élémens du Chant.
Lascelles (née Catley), Anne: The Life of Miss Anne Catley.
Mainwaring, John: Memoirs of the Life of the Late George Frederic Handel
Malcolm, Alexander: A Treaty of Music: Speculative, Practical and Historical
Marx, Adolph Bernhard: Die Kunst des Gesanges, Theoretisch-Practisch
May, Florence: The Life of Brahms
May, Florence: The Girlhood Of Clara Schumann: Clara Wieck And Her Time.
Mellers, Wilfrid: Angels of the Night: Popular Female Singers of Our Time
Mellers, Wilfrid: Bach and the Dance of God
Mellers, Wilfrid: Beethoven and the Voice of God
Mellers, Wilfrid: Caliban Reborn - Renewal in Twentieth Century Music
Mellers, Wilfrid: Darker Shade of Pale, A Backdrop to Bob Dylan

Music and Books published by Travis & Emery Music Bookshop:

Mellers, Wilfrid: François Couperin and the French Classical Tradition
Mellers, Wilfrid: Harmonious Meeting
Mellers, Wilfrid: Le Jardin Retrouvé, The Music of Frederic Mompou
Mellers, Wilfrid: Music and Society, England and the European Tradition
Mellers, Wilfrid: Music in a New Found Land: ... ... American Music
Mellers, Wilfrid: Romanticism and the Twentieth Century (from 1800)
Mellers, Wilfrid: The Masks of Orpheus: ...... the Story of European Music.
Mellers, Wilfrid: The Sonata Principle (from c. 1750)
Mellers, Wilfrid: Vaughan Williams and the Vision of Albion
Panchianio, Cattuffio: Rutzvanscad Il Giovine
Pearce, Charles: Sims Reeves, Fifty Years of Music in England.
Playford, John: An Introduction to the Skill of Musick.
Purcell, Henry et al: Harmonia Sacra ... The First Book, (1726)
Purcell, Henry et al: Harmonia Sacra ... Book II (1726)
Quantz, Johann: Versuch einer Anweisung die Flöte trave rsiere zu spielen.
Rameau, Jean-Philippe: Code de Musique Pratique, ou Methodes.
Rameau, Jean-Philippe: Erreurs sur La Musique dans l'Encyclopédie
Rastall, Richard: The Notation of Western Music.
Rimbault, Edward: The Pianoforte, Its Origins, Progress, and Construction.
Rousseau, Jean Jacques: Dictionnaire de Musique
Rubinstein, Anton : Guide to the proper use of the Pianoforte Pedals.
Sainsbury, John S.: Dictionary of Musicians. (1825). 2 vols.
Serré de Rieux, Jean de : Les dons des Enfans de Latone
Simpson, Christopher: A Compendium of Practical Musick in Five Parts
Spohr, Louis: Autobiography
Spohr, Louis: Grand Violin School
Tans'ur, William: A New Musical Grammar; or The Harmonical Spectator
Terry, Charles Sanford: Bach's Chorals – Parts 1, 2 and 3.
Terry, Charles Sanford: John Christian Bach
Terry, Charles Sanford: J.S. Bach's Original Hymn-Tunes for Congregational Use.
Terry, Charles Sanford: Four-Part Chorals of J.S. Bach. (German & English)
Terry, Charles Sanford: Joh. Seb. Bach, Cantata Texts, Sacred and Secular.
Terry, Charles Sanford: The Origins of the Family of Bach Musicians.
Tosi, Pierfrancesco: Opinioni de' Cantori Antichi, e Moderni
Tosi, Pierfrancesco: Observations on the Florid Song.
Van der Straeten, Edmund: History of the Violoncello, The Viol da Gamba ...
Van der Straeten, Edmund: History of the Violin, Its Ancestors... (2 vols.)
Walther, J. G. [Waltern]: Musicalisches Lexikon [Musikalisches Lexicon]
Wagner, Richard: Beethoven (Leipzig 1870)
Wagner, Richard: Lebens-Bericht (Leipzig 1884)
Wagner, Richard: The Musaic of the Future (Translated by E. Dannreuther).
Zwirn, Gerald: Stranded Stories From The Operas

Travis & Emery Music Bookshop
17 Cecil Court, London, WC2N 4EZ, United Kingdom.
Tel. (+44) 20 7240 2129

Discographies by Travis & Emery:
Discographies by John Hunt.

1987: 978-1-906857-14-1: From Adam to Webern: the Recordings of von Karajan.

1991: 978-0-951026-83-0: 3 Italian Conductors and 7 Viennese Sopranos: 10 Discographies: Arturo Toscanini, Guido Cantelli, Carlo Maria Giulini, Elisabeth Schwarzkopf, Irmgard Seefried, Elisabeth Gruemmer, Sena Jurinac, Hilde Gueden, Lisa Della Casa, Rita Streich.

1992: 978-0-951026-85-4: Mid-Century Conductors and More Viennese Singers: 10 Discographies: Karl Boehm, Victor De Sabata, Hans Knappertsbusch, Tullio Serafin, Clemens Krauss, Anton Dermota, Leonie Rysanek, Eberhard Waechter, Maria Reining, Erich Kunz.

1993: 978-0-951026-87-8: More 20th Century Conductors: 7 Discographies: Eugen Jochum, Ferenc Fricsay, Carl Schuricht, Felix Weingartner, Josef Krips, Otto Klemperer, Erich Kleiber.

1994: 978-0-951026-88-5: Giants of the Keyboard: 6 Discographies: Wilhelm Kempff, Walter Gieseking, Edwin Fischer, Clara Haskil, Wilhelm Backhaus, Artur Schnabel.

1994: 978-0-951026-89-2: Six Wagnerian Sopranos: 6 Discographies: Frieda Leider, Kirsten Flagstad, Astrid Varnay, Martha Moedl, Birgit Nilsson, Gwyneth Jones.

1995: 978-0-952582-70-0: Musical Knights: 6 Discographies: Henry Wood, Thomas Beecham, Adrian Boult, John Barbirolli, Reginald Goodall, Malcolm Sargent.

1995: 978-0-952582-71-7: A Notable Quartet: 4 Discographies: Gundula Janowitz, Christa Ludwig, Nicolai Gedda, Dietrich Fischer-Dieskau.

1996: 978-0-952582-75-5: Leopold Stokowski (1882-1977): Discography and Concert Register

1996: 978-0-952582-76-2: Makers of the Philharmonia: 11 Discographies: Alceo Galliera, Walter Susskind, Paul Kletzki, Nicolai Malko, Issay Dobrowen, Lovro Von Matacic, Efrem Kurtz, Otto Ackermann, Anatole Fistoulari, George Weldon, Robert Irving.

1996: 978-0-952582-72-4: The Post-War German Tradition: 5 Discographies: Rudolf Kempe, Joseph Keilberth, Wolfgang Sawallisch, Rafael Kubelik, Andre Cluytens.

1996: 978-0-952582-73-1: Teachers and Pupils: 7 Discographies: Elisabeth Schwarzkopf, Maria Ivoguen, Maria Cebotari, Meta Seinemeyer, Ljuba Welitsch, Rita Streich, Erna Berger.

1996: 978-0-952582-75-5: Leopold Stokowski: Discography and Concert Listing.

1996: 978-0-952582-76-2: Makers of the Philharmonia: 11 Discographies Alceo Galliera, Walter Susskind, Paul Kletzki, Nicolai Malko, Issay Dobrowen, Lovro Von Matacic, Efrem Kurtz, Otto Ackermann, Anatole Fistoulari, George Weldon, Robert Irving.

1996: 978-0-952582-77-9: Tenors in a Lyric Tradition: 3 Discographies: Peter Anders, Walther Ludwig, Fritz Wunderlich.

1997: 978-0-952582-78-6: The Lyric Baritone: 5 Discographies: Hans Reinmar, Gerhard Huesch, Josef Metternich, Hermann Uhde, Eberhard Waechter.

1997: 978-0-952582-79-3: Hungarians in Exile: 3 Discographies: Fritz Reiner, Antal Dorati, George Szell.

1997: 978-1-901395-00-6: The Art of the Diva: 3 Discographies: Claudia Muzio, Maria Callas, Magda Olivero.

1997: 978-1-901395-01-3: Metropolitan Sopranos: 4 Discographies: Rosa Ponselle, Eleanor Steber, Zinka Milanov, Leontyne Price.

1997: 978-1-901395-02-0: Back From The Shadows: 4 Discographies: Willem Mengelberg, Dimitri Mitropoulos, Hermann Abendroth, Eduard Van Beinum.

1997: 978-1-901395-03-7: More Musical Knights: 4 Discographies: Hamilton Harty, Charles Mackerras, Simon Rattle, John Pritchard.

1998: 978-1-901395-95-2: More Giants of the Keyboard: 5 Discographies: Claudio Arrau, Gyorgy Cziffra, Vladimir Horowitz, Dinu Lipatti, Artur Rubinstein.

1998: 978-1-901395-94-5: Conductors On The Yellow Label: 8 Discographies: Fritz Lehmann, Ferdinand Leitner, Ferenc Fricsay, Eugen Jochum, Leopold Ludwig, Artur Rother, Franz Konwitschny, Igor Markevitch.

1998: 978-1-901395-96-9: Mezzo and Contraltos: 5 Discographies: Janet Baker, Margarete Klose, Kathleen Ferrier, Giulietta Simionato, Elisabeth Hoengen.

1999: 978-1-901395-97-6: The Furtwaengler Sound Sixth Edition: Discography and Concert Listing.

1999: 978-1-901395-98-3: The Great Dictators: 3 Discographies: Evgeny Mravinsky, Artur Rodzinski, Sergiu Celibidache.

1999: 978-1-901395-99-0: Sviatoslav Richter: Pianist of the Century: Discography.

2000: 978-1-901395-04-4: Philharmonic Autocrat 1: Discography of: Herbert Von Karajan [Third Edition].

2000: 978-1-901395-05-1: Wiener Philharmoniker 1 - Vienna Philharmonic and Vienna State Opera Orchestras: Discography Part 1 1905-1954.

2000: 978-1-901395-06-8: Wiener Philharmoniker 2 - Vienna Philharmonic and Vienna State Opera Orchestras: Discography Part 2 1954-1989.

2001: 978-1-901395-07-5: Gramophone Stalwarts: 3 Separate Discographies: Bruno Walter, Erich Leinsdorf, Georg Solti.

2001: 978-1-901395-08-2: Singers of the Third Reich: 5 Discographies: Helge Roswaenge, Tiana Lemnitz, Franz Voelker, Maria Mueller, Max Lorenz.

2001: 978-1-901395-09-9: Philharmonic Autocrat 2: Concert Register of Herbert Von Karajan Second Edition.

2002: 978-1-901395-10-5: Sächsische Staatskapelle Dresden: Complete Discography.

2002: 978-1-901395-11-2: Carlo Maria Giulini: Discography and Concert Register.

2002: 978-1-901395-12-9: Pianists For The Connoisseur: 6 Discographies: Arturo Benedetti Michelangeli, Alfred Cortot, Alexis Weissenberg, Clifford Curzon, Solomon, Elly Ney.

2003: 978-1-901395-14-3: Singers on the Yellow Label: 7 Discographies: Maria Stader, Elfriede Troetschel, Annelies Kupper, Wolfgang Windgassen, Ernst Haefliger, Josef Greindl, Kim Borg.

2003: 978-1-901395-15-0: A Gallic Trio: 3 Discographies: Charles Muench, Paul Paray, Pierre Monteux.

2004: 978-1-901395-16-7: Antal Dorati 1906-1988: Discography and Concert Register.

2004: 978-1-901395-17-4: Columbia 33CX Label Discography.

2004: 978-1-901395-18-1: Great Violinists: 3 Discographies: David Oistrakh, Wolfgang Schneiderhan, Arthur Grumiaux.

2006: 978-1-901395-19-8: Leopold Stokowski: Second Edition of the Discography.

2006: 978-1-901395-20-4: Wagner Im Festspielhaus: Discography of the Bayreuth Festival.

2006: 978-1-901395-21-1: Her Master's Voice: Concert Register and Discography of Dame Elisabeth Schwarzkopf [Third Edition].

2007: 978-1-901395-22-8: Hans Knappertsbusch: Kna: Concert Register and Discography of Hans Knappertsbusch, 1888-1965. Second Edition.

2008: 978-1-901395-23-5: Philips Minigroove: Second Extended Version of the European Discography.

2009: 978-1-901395-24-2: American Classics: The Discographies of Leonard Bernstein and Eugene Ormandy.

2010: 978-1-901395-25-9: Dirigenten der DDR: Conductors of the German Democratic Republic

Discography by Stephen J. Pettitt, edited by John Hunt:

1987: 978-1-906857-16-5: Philharmonia Orchestra: Complete Discography 1945-1987

Available from: Travis & Emery at 17 Cecil Court, London, UK. (+44) 20 7 240 2129. email on sales@travis-and-emery.com .